The
DACHSHUND

EDITED BY
JUDY SQUIRES & IAN SEATH

BEST of
BREED

ACKNOWLEDGEMENTS
The publishers would like to thank the following for help with photography: Sally Mutch; Rosy Clifford (Ablebody); Ian and Sue Seath (Sunsong); Zena Thorn Andrews (Drakesleat); Jason Hunt (Carpaccio); Carole Worswick (Dolyharp); Pat Endersby (Mowbray); Sue Burke (Bonavoir); Sally Ann Thompson; Hearing Dogs for Deaf People; Pets As Therapy.

Cover photo: © Tracy Morgan Animal Photography (www.animalphotographer.co.uk)
Dog featured is Sunsong Sea Mist, owned by Sue Seath.

Pages 12 and 15 © Linda Brown (Garbosa Mini Longs); Page 121 © istockphoto.com/Mark Herreid

The British Breed Standard reproduced in Chapter 7 is the copyright of the Kennel Club and published with the Club's kind permission. Extracts from the American Breed Standard are reproduced by kind permission of the American Kennel Club.

THE QUESTION OF GENDER
**The 'he' pronoun is used throughout this book instead of the rather impersonal 'it',
but no gender bias is intended.**

First published in 2011 by The Pet Book Publishing Company Limited
PO Box 8, Lydney, Gloucestershire GL15 6YD

ISBN
978-1-906305-45-1
1-906305-45-5

Printed and bound in China through Printworks Int. Ltd.

CONTENTS

GETTING TO KNOW DACHSHUNDS

Chapter 1

Throughout the years, the British Royal Family has been admirers and owners of the Dachshund; it is said that they have been in the Royal Household since at least 1840 when Prince Albert brought two to England. They were of the Smooth-haired variety as the Long-haired and Wire-haired came to Britain later. The Queen Mother was the owner of Miniature Smooth-haired Dachshunds for a number of years and, up until her death, was an honorary life member of the Dachshund Club.

Due to the Dachshund being associated with Germany, Waldi the Dachshund was the mascot of the Munich 1972 Summer Olympic Games, and, in the early Micky Mouse comics, Micky had a Dachshund called Weenie. The author P.G. Wodehouse owned Jed and film stars Clark Gable,

Carole Lombard, Joan Crawford, Marlon Brando and John Wayne were all proud owners of Dachshunds. Lump, German for rascal, was the pet of the artist Pablo Picasso and he was thought to have inspired some of Picasso's work. Andy Warhol owned Amos and Archie, and David Hockney has immortalised on canvas his Dachshunds, Stanley and Boogie.

The breed's distinctive shape has led to it being caricatured and the butt of numerous jokes, especially when it is portrayed as a comical, obese and elongated dog on short legs – hence the slang name "sausage dog". Nothing could be further from the truth. This is a dog that is instantly recognisable with personality, intelligence and imbued with a great sense of humour. The American author Robert S. Lemmon said of them that they are: "Half a dog high, a

dog and a half long and three dogs in the matter of brains".

Whatever size they may be – Standard or Miniature – they are faithful and good-tempered, full of self-importance, loyal, dignified and keenly independent. In other words, this is a breed that is full of character. Whether you are a town or country dweller, if you want to share your life with a dog of moderate size with all these attributes, plus being an intelligent hound with sporting instincts and a good nose, then look no further. A Dachshund is an outstanding companion who will be at your side for 12 or more years.

BREED CHARACTERISTICS
The Dachshund will adapt to town or country living but, perhaps, the Miniature variety is better for the town. If you are a town dweller, you must satisfy his sporting instincts with a long

This is a sporting breed that should be kept fit in mind and body.

walk in the park if you are able, as this is a good alternative to pounding the streets. After puppyhood, the average Standard will require to be exercised about an hour each day and the Miniature for half an hour minimum. However, once fully mature, both sizes will take as much exercise as you can give them – and you are likely to want to go home before they do.

If you are a keen gardener then you must bear in mind that a Dachshund loves to dig. Therefore, your garden should be well fenced and, ideally, fencing should be buried securely in the ground so that your dog has no chance of digging his way out. He can be obstinate, like most hounds, and he has a habit of "turning a deaf ear" when spoken to. This means he will, more likely than not, only do what he wants to do when he is ready and not before.

Dachshunds are excellent house dogs and will guard your property from any unwelcome guests. His bark can be deep, especially in Standards, and people are often surprised to hear such a deep noise coming from a dog the size of a Dachshund.

A Dachshund will be good with children and can become a devoted pal and playmate, as long as the children are brought up to respect him and do not tease him in any way. He will also live quite happily with the family cat, but out of the home it is usually a different matter – any outside cat is considered an intruder and will be chased with glee.

When you start to train your Dachshund you may find him rather self-willed, so he requires firm leadership. However, this does not mean rough handling. A Dachshund needs to be praised and encouraged in what you want him to do. You will find that he responds to your voice, and with the offer of a morsel of food, you will get the most from him.

All Dachshunds love their food and will eat almost anything and everything that is placed before them, plus a few extras that they may find. So do not pander to those pleading eyes, as there is nothing worse than an obese dog, especially a Dachshund. It is

THE SMOOTH-HAIRED DACHSHUND
AN EXPERT'S VIEW
Edna Cooper (Sontag)

The first Smooth-haired Dachshund I met was holidaying with a neighbour who lived in the flat upstairs. It was love at first meeting. It was his character that captivated me; he was such a snooty chap until he decided he liked me. If I had to choose one word to describe a Smooth, I would suggest 'astute'. In my dictionary the definition is: discerning, ingenious, intelligent, quick, sharp, and shrewd.

Smooths are ideal for anyone who likes the wash-and-go variety of dog that needs very little work to take him in the show ring. The downside is: no judicial coat trimming to cover up any faults. Good-quality food and regular exercise are needed to produce a shining coat and tight, bunched feet.

Smooth Dachshund registrations and entries at shows have been declining steadily since I started to show them in the mid-1970s. This seems to be the trend in all three Standard varieties, while the Miniature varieties enjoy much higher registrations and entries at shows. I wonder if this has anything to do with today's lifestyle where modern houses are smaller; smaller dogs do not need as much exercise and anyone keeping several, as most exhibitors do, can accommodate more Miniatures in the same amount of space.

Smooth coats have improved over the years; there are very few bald ears and tails to be seen nowadays. Temperament is much the same, some show dogs cooperating if you insist, others looking as if they are having a lovely day out.

Large kennels of the mid-1990s have all but disappeared. Fortunately, there is still a small but devoted following of Smooth exhibitors and hobby breeders who enjoy the competitive spirit around the ring. I still get a thrill to see a good example of our variety. Standard Smooth Dachshunds regularly take top honours and can still hold their own against competition from the other five varieties.

THE MINIATURE SMOOTH-HAIRED DACHSHUND AN EXPERT'S VIEW

Lovaine Coxon (D'Arisca)

It is a widely held belief that the Smooth-haired Dachshund was the first and original of the six breeds of Dachshund to arrive in the United Kingdom. Smooth Dachshunds come in two sizes – Miniature and Standard. On the continent there is a third size, Kaninchen, which means 'rabbit', and they are very small.

The Miniature Smooth-haired Dachshund is a small but elegant dog with a coat that takes very little effort to keep in gleaming condition. Rain or mud or slime, not to mention other unsavoury substances that are attractive to all dogs, will fall away from his sleek body.

However, a Miniature Smooth-haired Dachshund does need a regular manicure to keep his very strong nails neat. Regular teeth cleaning is essential to ensure that he does not develop gum problems. Always check his ears after running through long grass to ensure that grass seeds have not got lodged into the ear canal. Seeds can create serious problems if left undetected in the ear.

When choosing a Miniature Smooth-haired Dachshund as a family pet, it is most important to take time to find a responsible breeder who specialises in the breed – someone who will have reared their puppies to the highest standards and who appreciates the value of socialisation for puppies. Always ask a breeder of Miniature Smooth Dachshunds if they have had the parents of your puppy tested for a condition called the *cord 1 PRA* mutation. Eye testing the parents will ensure that you have bought a puppy that will not develop the condition.

Although Miniature Dachshunds are small dogs, they behave as though they are much larger. They should have a very strong frame and have a well-covered body without carrying excess fat. This can sometimes be difficult to achieve, as a Dachshund is a very greedy dog.

Having lived with Dachshunds of all sizes and all coats for more than 50 years, you could be forgiven for thinking that I like them. You would be wrong, because I simply adore them!

just as cruel to have an overweight dog as a very thin and undernourished one, as both extremes can be detrimental to general health.

Although the Dachshund is a moderately long and low dog compared with other breeds, he is a sporting dog and not a lap dog. His original purpose in life was to enter badger sets or rabbit warrens, so he must be kept fit in body and mind if you wish to retain some of the breed characteristics that drew you to him in the first instance. Saying that, he is adaptable and loves nothing better than having a cuddle or curling up in the front of the fire, especially if it is raining!

BUYING PUPPIES

There are dozens of books about pure-bred dogs to be found in bookshops and every local library in this country. All will have a chapter offering advice on how to choose a puppy – but I would like to look at this from a different angle.

Prospective puppy buyers should think of the mother of their eventual choice of a family pet. The mother plays a crucial role in the early life of every puppy.

When you go to see puppies with a view to buying one, please insist on seeing their mother. Watch how she responds to the puppies and how the puppies respond to her. Insist on learning where she produced and reared her babies and do not be put off by any excuses. Remember, only

Make sure you see the puppies with their mother.

a happy and well-cared-for bitch, with good experiences of people, will produce well-balanced puppies who will trust and like us.

THE SIX VARIETIES

There are two sizes of Dachshund to choose from. Firstly, the Standard Dachshund, which should weigh no more than 26 lbs (12 kgs) and secondly, the Miniature Dachshund, which should, ideally, weigh 10 lbs (4.5 kgs) and no more than 11 lbs (5 kgs). These two sizes can be found in Smooth-haired, Long-haired and Wire-haired coats, so basically there are six varieties of Dachshund available, all, more or less, having similar temperaments and characteristics as mentioned earlier. Of course, there can be slight variations, but this is more dependent on their rearing and the temperament coming through

from past generations, as can be seen in any breed of dog.

COLOUR

Not only are there six varieties to choose from – each variety comes in a range of colours. The Breed Standard states that all colours are allowed, as long as large patches of white do not predominate.

COAT

- The Smooth-haired varieties are covered in a short, dense, strong coat.
- The Long-haired has a soft, shiny coat that can be straight or slightly waved, giving the dog an appearance of elegance.
- The Wire-haired should be covered in a short, harsh, straight coat with a dense undercoat. There should be a beard on the chin and bushy eyebrows, but the hair on the ears should be almost smooth.

DACHSHUND COLOURS

LONG-HAIRED

Shaded Red

Black and Tan.

MINIATURE LONG-HAIRED

Brindle.

Dapple.

Left to right: Shaded Cream, Red, Cream.

SMOOTH-HAIRED

Chocolate and Tan.

MINIATURE SMOOTH-HAIRED

Black and Tan.

Red.

WIRE-HAIRED

Brindle (left) and Chocolate and Tan.

MINIATURE WIRE-HAIRED

Left to right: Chocolate and Tan, Brindle (Wild Boar), Black and Tan, Grey Brindle.

THE LONG-HAIRED DACHSHUND
AN EXPERT'S VIEW
Fran Mitchell (Bronia)

Long-haired Dachshunds are, to me, the perfect companion. They love a long walk, but on a rainy day they are very happy to stay indoors. In general, they are very laid-back in character; nothing bothers them and they are happy to join in any fun! They are, like the other varieties, selectively deaf when it comes to obeying orders, depending on whether or not they are ready to do your bidding.

Longs are the most glamorous of the varieties, with a very easy coat to care for. A quick brush through after exercise will get rid of any sand or dust, and a proper comb through with a steel comb twice a week, with special attention to behind the ears, under elbows and through the knickers, will ensure no mats develop. I bath my Longs about once every three weeks or so, just to keep them smelling fresh. I recommend a tea tree oil shampoo, which has the added bonus of repelling insects. This may be needed more often if your dog finds something pungent to roll in!

To have the coat kept in the very best condition, I use mink oil spray every week when I am grooming, as it brings out a wonderful shine to his coat. It is wise to learn how to keep your dog's feet tidy, by cutting the excess hair from under his pads and in between his toes; a dog will not look his best when wearing carpet slippers!

Longs are in a healthy position at the moment with no known inherited genetic disorders. Plenty of new bloodlines have been introduced from America, Australia and Europe in recent years, so the gene pool is quite diverse. Hopefully, this healthy state of affairs will continue long into the future. Construction is sound and, with temperaments that are very loving, the Longs have a lot to offer as family pets.

Whatever you want a Long to learn is easily taken on board, but you must be firm and clear in your commands and, remember, practice makes perfect. Puppies need to know that you are the leader and be persuaded to co-operate. With Longs, I find reward tactics are usually the most successful.

A Long-haired Dachshund is a very handsome dog with a very good nature. Ask your breeder for guidance, or you could get in touch with your breed club secretary so you can be in touch with like-minded Long-haired Dachshund lovers.

THE MINIATURE LONG HAIRED DACHSHUND AN EXPERT'S VIEW

Ruth Lockett-Walters (Ralines)

The original variety of Dachshund I had the pleasure of owning was a Standard Smooth-haired, with which I had much success in the show ring. However, due to family circumstances I wished to continue with my hobby but required a smaller variety that was different and would present me with a new challenge. I opted for the Miniature Long-haired variety, which, in many respects, is very different to its larger Smooth-coated cousins.

The Miniature Long is very sweet-tempered. This variety has a very loving nature – especially the boys – and is very much a convenience breed to own. The Miniature Long still has that hound instinct and he can be a game little hunter. He is assertive, makes a wonderful guard dog and is endlessly inquisitive. He also has a lovely soft, gentle side, which makes him an ideal family pet.

Some pet owners are put off by the coat, but this is not a problem. A Long-haired Dachshund, be it a Miniature or a Standard, should not have a profuse amount of coat. He should have a flat body coat and feathering on the chest, legs and tail. The coat is waterproof and dries very quickly when rubbed briskly with a towel.

Unfortunately, the Mini Long became very popular because of the exotic colours you could obtain: for example, creams (many people call them blondes) and dapples. Due to this popularity of different colours, the variety became subject to unscrupulous breeders who bred purely for profit, and many breeders were unaware that we had an inherited eye problem in our variety.

In recent years, thanks to the help of the Animal Heath Trust and dedicated breed lovers, we have been able to set up a DNA testing scheme for our variety. It is therefore imperative, when purchasing a puppy, that you ascertain whether his parents have been DNA tested for the PRA (cord1) eye disease. Hopefully, after several years of dedication by responsible breeders, this defect is now well on the way to being eradicated.

Finally, when purchasing a Dachshund of any variety you must remember that he is a little hound on small legs. This being so, they need to be kept fit, not fat, and never encouraged to sit up and beg, because of the length of their back. Miniature Long-hairs are, by and large, healthy, active little dogs and should be treated as such. They are most definitely not lap dogs.

THE WIRE-HAIRED DACHSHUND
AN EXPERT'S VIEW
Lesley Patton (Lesandnic)

I love Wires for their sheer adaptability – they are literally the go-anywhere, do-anything dog. There is no walk too far or too difficult, yet no bed too soft for a Wire-haired Dachshund. My top tip for any new owner is to make sure you get the most from your Wire – ensure he is part of the family and is involved in everything.

Take your dog with you wherever you go – even a car trip to the supermarket is fun – but don't leave your shopping unattended, as you may come back to a lot less of it! The only possible disadvantage of a Wire-haired Dachshund is his ability to find something he thinks is edible and eat it in large quantities!

Do not listen to anyone who tells you Dachshunds are not obedient. They can be obedient when they want to be, and they are very clever, so training them in any sphere – obedience, tracking, agility – is more than worthwhile. Oh, and they adore dog shows; anyone who doubts this is welcome to watch what happens in our house when we are packing the car for a show.

Type differences around the world are becoming less obvious, with the exception of size and condition, and good Wires from any country can, and do, win anywhere. British Wires at present excel in heads and front assemblies. Over the last 30 years, hind angulation has altered. There is a tendency now towards over-angulation – and a consequent lack in soundness – so we need to pay attention to improving hind movement. Coats are mostly still of the 'need tidying' type, but a few minutes of daily attention with a brush, comb, and finger and thumb keeps most looking in good order. Any slight tendency towards exaggerated 'longness' and 'lowness' should be corrected by the new Breed Standard. We are aiming for a moderately long dog, and the length should come from the ribbing rather than the loin.

The Breed Standard states that size can range from 9-12 kgs (20-26 lbs), but a 10 kg (22 lb) Wire can look very small in the UK ring. This is not helped by the fact that many British Dachshunds carry rather more weight than they should. I have always believed that you should be able to carry a Standard Dachshund under each arm – this is a very helpful way of checking size! Chests tend to be too deep. The Breed Standard now states "enough ground clearance to allow free movement", so we should see an end to dogs appearing to have no legs in grass, and, hopefully, an end to judges praising "lovely deep chests".

The Dachshund retains strong hunting instincts.

HEALTH AND WELFARE

The health and welfare of all pedigree dogs is the top priority of national kennel clubs, and in recent years, the emphasis has been placed ever more strongly on this, in the belief that every dog should be bred to be fit enough to enjoy a long, happy, healthy life. The breed clubs also work tirelessly on this issue.

The vast majority of Dachshund breeders care very deeply about the health and welfare of their dogs and wish to put an end to the unethical puppy farming trade. This is why we want to impress on you that you must be able to recognise which are reputable breeders and which are the ones you need to avoid. So, when you are ready to purchase your Dachshund, or any

breed, in fact, it is essential you either speak to your local vet or contact the Kennel Club and/or one of the Dachshund clubs.

Dachshunds generally suffer from few health problems and are long-lived, provided they are kept well exercised, fit and are fed a healthy, balanced diet. But like any pedigree or crossbreed dog, they can be susceptible to inherited diseases. Currently, there is a DNA test for an inherited eye condition that affects some Miniature Dachshunds. *For details of this and other matters regarding health, see Chapter 8.*

WORKING ORIGINS

The origin of the Dachshund has been debated for many years by knowledgeable breeders, but one

thing is certain – it has been a sporting breed for centuries. The Dachshund has excelled in tracking for their work underground and for badger hunting. Their conformation of a long body and oval ribcage, allowing plenty of heart and lung capacity, enables them to work well underground.

Dachshunds were used to dig and drive out the badgers from their sett for the waiting huntsmen with their guns. Badgers make fierce opponents, especially when cornered, so a Dachshund had to possess powerful jaws and a great deal of courage to confront them. They are still widely used in Germany to go to ground after a fox and draw it out for the waiting hounds and guns. They are also

THE MINIATURE WIRE-HAIRED DACHSHUND
AN EXPERT'S VIEW
Jeff Horswell (Drakesleat)

Although the Miniature Wire was the last of the current six varieties to be established in the UK, it quickly gained popularity. It was a great benefit that many of the people who took up the variety were already well-established Dachshund breeders and this must have helped us to gain CC status so quickly. Mini Wires also had great appeal to people in other breeds, many of whom have successfully added the Mini Wire to their kennel.

It is easy to see why this variety has such great appeal. The Mini Wire is a big dog in a small frame. Tough and hardy, he fits in well with other breeds, keeping up on walks and often leading the pack. The Mini Wire has cute, good looks, with the most endearing wicked expression, and a wonderful temperament. He has a "busy-ness" that other varieties do not have, no doubt due in part to the breeds introduced to produce the Wire coat.

It is the coat makes him a great, all-weather dog, able to go through the thickest of cover, in any weather.

The quality of the Mini Wire has always been diverse. We have always attracted some very clever breeders, and our best have taken on the best of other breeds in the show ring. Sadly, at the present time, I feel they lack a depth of quality and consistency of type. Some look more like a toy breed and others are inclined to the terrier, especially in the front assembly. The correct Dachshund front has to be bred for.

However, I think the Mini Wire variety does, in the main, lack the exaggeration of some of the other varieties, and size is certainly a lot more consistent now than in years past. Coats have also improved.

My top tip for anyone serious about our wonderful breed is to watch all six varieties, and not just in the UK. Have an open mind, try to appreciate correct Dachshund type, and remember that this is a small Dachshund with a Wire coat, not a 'Mini Wire'.

Photo © Carol Ann Johnson.

used in areas of undergrowth to track wounded game and deer, and it is said that they have the scenting power of a Foxhound. In Germany, the Miniature variety has long been appreciated and small specimens, bred from normal-sized parents, appeared from time to time and were used to go into rabbit burrows or enter earths of other animals that were too narrow for larger dogs.

FIRST BREED STANDARDS

On the 7 January 1881 a number of gentlemen, who were the most successful owners and exhibitors of Dachshunds of the time, met at the Cox's Hotel, Jermyn Street, London, to form the Dachshund Club. With Mr Montague Wootten as the first honorary secretary, they set about drawing up a Standard of Points based on their ideas of what the breed should look like and what breeders should aim for. This was, of course, based on the dogs they knew and owned. They had only their own ideas as a guideline, as the German Dachshund Club did not come into fruition until seven years later.

It is amazing to realise that this Standard included a great many good points that were considered a few years later – and even now – as not desirable in the Dachshund.

In 1888 the German Dachshund Club was formed and produced its own Standard of Points, which differed in many ways from the English version. The English Standard stayed in

place for the next 16 years, although the winning show stock that were brought in from Germany also won with equal honours on the show scene in England, as they were very similar in type. Due to this, in 1907 the Dachshund Club recommended that the English Standard be revised in order to conform more closely to the German Standard. This remained in place until 1986 when the English Standard was revised again to cover all the six varieties. Since that time there have been a few amendments made, the latest revision being in 2009.

Dachshunds were, and still are, popular in America. They first appeared in the American Kennel Club Stud Book of 1885, which would indicate that there had been several importations from Europe some years earlier.

BREED STANDARD TODAY

Every breed of pedigree dog that is registered at the Kennel Club has a Breed Standard. These are owned by the Kennel Club and are drawn up after an in-depth discussion with the relevant clubs. It is a blueprint of how the ideal Dachshund should look and move, and also gives information on temperament and the breed's original use. It is important that when breeders strive to produce the ideal Dachshund in looks, the character, temperament and health must also be uppermost in breeders' minds. A Dachshund should retain everything that is required to make a wonderful pet animal, and also do well in the

show ring. *For more information on the Breed Standard, see Chapter Seven.*

REGISTRATIONS

Dachshunds have grown in popularity since they started to be imported from Germany in the middle of the 19th century and increased steadily in the years before the First World War. The war caused a severe setback to the breed, partly due to the difficulty of keeping dogs because of food shortages and partly due to the anti-German sentiment towards the Dachshund.

In 1918 the Kennel Club registrations for Dachshunds had fallen to nine but soon after the war there were 30 registered in 1920 and 185 by 1924. Luckily, they were not affected much by the Second World War and registrations of the Standard variety increased steadily. This has continued right up to the present day, when all six varieties of Dachshund, collectively, remain as one of the most popular breeds in the UK.

Most early registrations in the 20th century were for Standard Dachshunds with just a few Miniature Dachshunds. But it was not long before Miniatures started growing in popularity both for showing and for pets. The Miniature Club was formed in 1935 solely for the betterment of all coats of the Miniature Dachshund. The club wanted breeders to maintain the look and characteristics of their larger cousins: in other words, to breed a Standard in Miniature. It was

Therapy dogs can bring great joy to residents of nursing homes and hospitals.

also stressed that the Miniature was not a toy dog but a small hound. Their popularity has increased over the years, probably partly due to general lifestyles and partly due to people being able to keep them in towns as well as the countryside. Since the 1970s the Standards have declined in numbers, especially the Standard Smooth-haired, and many have also increased in size and weight beyond the desired weight given in the Breed Standard.

There have been a few fluctuations in Kennel Club registrations over the years, but out of all the Dachshunds it is the Miniature varieties that have the largest number of registrations, with the Miniature Smooth-haired now leading the way over the Miniature Long-haired, which was the most popular for many years. In the Standards it is the reverse situation, with the Standard Smooth-haired having the fewest dogs registered, followed closely by the Longs, and with the Wires heading the list in popularity.

DACHSHUNDS TODAY
All the six varieties of Dachshund make up more or less a third of the Hound Group registrations with the Kennel Club. The Dachshund is a very popular dog to own, especially the Miniatures which have gained in popularity with the general public.

Registrations in both the UK and the USA have increased at a steady rate due to the dedication of breeders to move with the times and to continue to breed healthy, happy animals that conform to the Breed Standard for showing, working and as pets. The responsible breeders have brought in plenty of new bloodlines from America, Canada, Australia and Europe to extend the gene pool for the good of the breed.

COMPANION DOGS
There are many roles your Dachshund can fulfil but, first and foremost, he will be your friend and loyal companion. That is why his popularity as a family

You may have ambitions to compete for honours in the show ring.

pet has not diminished over the years. The Dachshund today can be simply a pet within your household or he can undertake other roles during his life. You could perhaps attend one of the fun days that some Dachshund clubs put on, where your dog can go over small agility courses and generally have a good time.

THERAPY DOGS

Some Dachshunds are used as therapy dogs, where dog and owner visit people in hospices, care homes and schools, enabling people of all ages to reap the benefits brought by contact with dogs even though they may not be able to keep a dog of their own. This brings great joy into their lives, and you and your Dachshund will also reap happiness and a great deal of satisfaction from the visits. First, though, he will have to pass an assessment to make sure he has the right temperament to undertake these visits.

SHOW DOGS

Most dogs, when they are not from a large showing kennel, are primarily house pets first and show dogs second. The time you spend in the show ring with your Dachshund is minimal compared with time at home.

If you decide you wish to buy a Dachshund for the show ring, then your approach must be different. A reliable breeder will sell you a puppy that has "show potential", as it cannot be guaranteed that he will turn out to be successful or even a future Champion. Whatever his show results, he will still remain a valuable member of your family.

For more information on buying a show puppy, see Chapter Three.

WORKING WITH TECKELS
Sue Holt and Bernd Kugow (Waldmeister Miniature Wires)

In Germany, the country of origin, Teckels (Dachshunds) of all coats and sizes are used for hunting. There are three sizes of Teckel: Kaninchen (rabbit), Zwerg (dwarf), and Normal (standard). Their girth is measured to confirm their size, and this directly relates to the prey that they hunt (rabbit, fox or badger). As well as flushing birds and vermin to the gun, and dispatching such nuisances as rats and mice, Teckels are trained to track wounded deer and find those that have fallen, giving a recognisable bark on finding the animal.

Firstly, you need to decide what you want to do with your dog. If you decide you want to train your dog to find, flush and retrieve game birds, he will need to have a soft mouth and it is not advisable also to train him to find and dispatch vermin. Similarly, if you want your dog to track wounded game, he must not be introduced to vermin, because for game tracking he needs to be quiet. Vermin hunters give tongue when they are on the scent of vermin and are not useful for tracking when firstly trained for vermin hunting. We train our Miniature Wire-haired Dachshunds for either vermin hunting or game bird flushing. The type of terrain we have access to is open moorland and, as such, lends itself to fox, hare, rats and a variety of game birds.

Dachshunds are not terriers and do not work like terriers. They use their intelligence and speed to outwit their prey – they do not look for a fight but they will stand their ground against the opposition if they have to. Dachshunds, no matter how well trained, are stubborn, and, if you do not catch them with the whistle quickly enough when they put up a hare, you can often be left waiting for a good 20 minutes until they give up the chase and return with their tongues hanging out!

SELECTING A PUPPY FOR WORK
It is always a difficult decision when choosing a show puppy from our litters because as well as displaying some promise for the show ring, they

In Germany, the Teckel is still used as a hunting dog.

have to possess instinct, have the ability to enter cover, prove they are not gun shy, and be steady around livestock. Lots of puppies that we have chosen as good for showing end up going to new homes because they do not develop the necessary instinct. Keeping them could mean that they would be in danger when the others are out working.

In our kennel, both sides of the coin are of equal importance – we have working dogs that we enjoy showing. From a very young age (four weeks onwards), we introduce our puppies to sights and smells to see if they show interest in a fox tail, a pheasant wing, and the ground where animals (rabbits, hare and fox) have

The Teckel is an independent worker, and this must be taken into consideration when training him.

just departed. We then lay a tripe trail, out of the puppy's sight, to see which ones will hit the trail, which ones run about aimlessly, and which ones just are not interested at all. In the whelping box, we have a tunnel to see which ones will go through and are not afraid of new things, in readiness for entering natural and artificial burrows.

GETTING STARTED

When we have decided which puppies are being run on, we introduce them to our six-metre-long (19.5 ft) training burrow in the garden, and we let Gino (our German dog) show the youngsters the ropes, as he was shown by his father. From around six weeks, the puppies go on to the moor in good weather and there we can assess their

willingness to enter cover, their enthusiasm and instinct to explore, and their need to seek out the smells and trails. This is quite unpredictable and some that are very comfortable at home can "freeze" up on the moor.

If gentle persuasion does not light their enthusiasm and interest, the puppy will not be kept by us, as the dogs must want to work and understand what it is they are looking for. It is not a case of running around and stumbling across something; a dog must know what to look for and how to look for it. Our dogs really understand what a fox smells like and, from quite early, will give tongue if they put up a fox or a hare.

For more information on training a Dachshund for working, see Chapter Six.

THE FIRST DACHSHUNDS

Chapter 2

Very short-legged dogs have been recognised for centuries. In fact, the name 'Dachshund' means 'badger dog'. 'Dachs' translates as 'badger' and 'hund' as 'dog'. As long as the Dachshund, or Dachshunde, has had this name, he has been a badger dog. We know he has been used as a sporting dog for several centuries, but it has not yet been proved conclusively which country he originated from.

Many 19th century writers put forward the idea that the Dachshund is merely a German edition of the French Basset Hound, and some 20th century writers have continued the story. Yes, some interchange of blood most certainly took place between the two breeds during the 18th and 19th centuries, and the early Dachshunds and Basset Hounds are very similar –

although not so alike as the Dachshund and certain terrier breeds. However, I do not believe that the Dachshund and the Basset are very strongly related. The evidence pointing this way is very slender indeed.

It was said that Basset Hounds were taken into German states by émigrés after the French Revolution in 1789, and it was only from this point onwards that the Dachshund was popular in what we now know as Germany. If this were true, it would imply there were no Dachshunds in Germany prior to the supposed Basset invasion. But we know that the breed was already in Germany, and was established well before the time of the French Revolution. It was even at this early time, acknowledged by some neighbouring countries as being of German origin.

The 19th century books featuring sections on dogs, such

as the *Sportsman's Cabinets* and *Companions, Repositories* etc, were generally compiled by men who enlarged fancifully on the very smallest threads of evidence. Serious research was not undertaken at this time, maybe with the exception of Mr G.H. Jesse, who wrote *The Researches into the History of the British Dog* in 1866. Other great authors, such as James Watson, Robert Leighton, and Edward Ash, certainly tried to solve the problem of the origin of the Dachshund, but they remained very cautious. Ash states in 1930: "The Dachshund is a breed which may have originated in Germany. As far as I can discover from searching through early books, the Dachshund was first mentioned in 1753, and first illustrated as a Dachshund in a German book in 1780."

The illustration he mentions must be the two Dachshunde by

There is evidence that low-to-ground dogs were used to hunt beaver and badger.

G. Riedel, the miniaturist painter employed by Dresden, published in Icones Animalium 1780. He actually names his picture *Dachshunde*. The well-known writer, historian and owner of the largest and most comprehensive dog book collection in the world, the late Clifford Hubbard, found an even earlier painting of a Smooth Dachshund named *Pehr* by Jean Baptist Oudry 1740, to illustrate the frontispiece of his *Dachshund Handbook* in 1950, from which I am indebted for these early references. *Pehr* was a black and tan dog and is portrayed sitting with a bag of game and a gun. This painting is in the National Museum of Sweden.

GATHERING EVIDENCE

Long-bodied and low-to-ground types of dogs were known in central Europe in the Middle Ages, and even earlier. A decree from King Dagobert in AD630 concerns just such a type of dog, telling us that this earth-going dog was used in hunting beaver and badger. Similar types of dogs were already in Britain, hunting beaver up to the 12th century. The earliest painting that we know of, showing this type of breed, is *The Vision of St. Eustace* painted in 1436 by Pisanello. This painting includes two Greyhounds, four to five medium hound-type breeds and, in the left foreground, two long-bodied low-to-ground dogs. This painting is in the National Gallery in London. These two early Dachshund types in this painting are busily tracking down a rabbit.

At the British Museum, there is a beautiful early 16th century calendar, showing the November scene as the return from a stag hunt. The six dogs present feature Greyhounds, Dachshund-type dogs and a rather larger hound type. The Dachs are coloured dark tan with lighter cheeks, bellies and the underside of the tails. The tails are gaily carried, but the head, ears and hind legs are very like the early Dachsbracke and Dachshunde.

In *The Dog in Art*, 1948, Hesketh Hubbard (a pseudonym for Clifford Hubbard) refers to the pictures of Teniers the Younger, who states: "I can recall a dog, short in leg and long in body that may have been a Dachshund or its prototype". Teniers was a painter of the Flemish school (1610-1694); yet more evidence that the Dachshund type was well known in Europe at this point in time.

Jacques du Fouilloux's *La Venerie*, 1560, was translated into German, Italian and English, with many woodcut illustrations. Two reproduced in the book show the type of dogs du Fouilloux called "Bassets", and Turberville in the English copy called "Terriers". In the first illustration, the dogs are going hunting, with a cart, accompanied by spades, howes (hoes) and matlocks, shovels, pickaxes, bottles and food – in fact, everything required for a successful day's hunting, including the servant girl kissing the head of her master in the cart!

A woodcut taken from *La Venarie*, 1560.

So we come to an extremely rare and desirable book, one copy of which I have seen but alas the price was beyond me! This book is *Cynographia Curiosa seu Canis Descriptio, 1685,* by Christiano Francisco Paullini. A well-known author who also wrote a book on wolves, he wrote this work in both German and Latin. The Dachshund is specifically referred to in several places in the text, including the following reference to the breeding of Miniatures. Clifford Hubbard translates this passage as follows.
"Give powdered nitrum, as much as remains on a moistened finger-tip, three or four times every morning to a bitch in whelp from a week before whelping and to the pups until six months old. This through its 'coldness' will prevent development and keep them quite small."

This book is so important to students of the breed, as it proves beyond any doubt that the breed was known by his present name in Germany in 1685.

THE 19TH CENTURY

There are many references to the breed and its varieties in the 19th century. Dr Leopold Fitzinger's highly-rated work *Der Hund und seine Racen,* 1876, tells us that no less than 12 varieties were recognised at this time. In J.H. Walsh's (Stonehenge) *The Dogs of the British Isles* (third edition, 1878) it is stated:
"… the Dachshund or German badger dog is generally considered in Germany to be a pure and independent breed, for a long time confined to the mountain chain and high forests of Southern and Central Europe, extending through Germany and into France, where he is probably the original of the Basset a Jambes torses. The old English Turnspit somewhat resembles him, but differs in his ears, which were more terrier-like, and also in his nose, which had even less of the hound character than that of the Dachshund."

From around 1860, the breed was imported into England and was largely sold by a Mr Schuller, who was responsible for the sale

Early photos of Smooth-haired Dachshunds in the *Ladies Kennel Journal*, 1895. These are Jocelyn II (dog) and Black Diamond (bitch). Both were owned by Mrs Firmstone.

of several hundred specimens. They were successfully bred by the Earl of Onslow, Mr Schweizer, and Mr Fisher, who was the most successful exhibitor of that time. Also prominent were the royal kennels and several small private kennels.

Stonehenge states that: "the breed has been well-tried in England as badger dogs, as well as for hare hunting". Opinions were divided as to their merits, some declaring that they were inferior to our own Beagles and Terriers, while others, including Mr Schweizer, maintained that "a good one would face any badger with as much pluck as our gamest terrier. The Dachshund is also used for driving deer to the gun, but for this purpose the straight-legged cross, *geradbeinige dachshund*, is most in demand, which variety is generally also larger in size and more hound-like in character."

These were probably from the spaniel-cross, which most likely produced the long-haired variety. Mr Schweizer states..

"In constitution the dog is hardy, but in temper somewhat wild and headstrong, so that he is often difficult to get under command when once on the scent. He is also snappish in kennel and inclined to fight on the slightest provocation, or often without it! His tongue is loud and shrill, without the deep bell note of the old-fashioned hound."

He goes on to say: "The best breeds are met within the vicinity of the Schwarzwald, Stuttgard, Lonberg, and Eberstein, near Baden Baden. Mr Fisher's celebrated dogs are from the kennels of Prince Edward of Saxe-Weimar".

The points of the Dachshund were at this time, described by the German Dachshund fanciers.

POINTS OF THE DACHSHUND

Skull	10
Legs	15
Colour	7½
Jaw	10
Feet	7½
Size, symmetry, and quality.	10
Ears, eyes, and lips	10
Stern	10
Length of body including neck	15

Vero Shaw's massive work, *The Illustrated Book of the Dog*, 1879-1881, was largely taken from Fitzinger's work, and deals with the Dachshund at length.

Major Emil Ilgner wrote the first book devoted entirely to the breed in 1896, thus *Der Dachshund* becomes a milestone in our breed history. It was closely followed by the huge British work of 1898, jointly written and compiled by E. Sydney Woodiwiss and E. Watlock Allen. This listed all the known pedigrees from the earliest

BREED CLUBS

The Kennel Club in Britain was formed in 1873, and brought out the first Stud Book (1859-1873) with all known show reports and pedigrees in 1874. This has been followed yearly right up to the present day. It is thought that the Dachshund Club is the oldest club in the UK, dating from 1881, but the Kennel Club only granted registration in 1891, along with several other specialist clubs. Dachshund Club members today are very proud to be part of this great tradition of nearly 130 years, devoted to this singular breed.

The German Teckel Club was formed in 1888 and celebrated its 100th birthday in 1988. Its Studbook or *Stammbuch* was first issued in 1890 with the pedigrees of 394 Dachshunds recorded for posterity. Just three were Wire-haired, five Long-haired and the other 386 were Smooth-haired Dachshunds. Miniatures did not appear separately in the studbook until 1900. There had been previous general studbooks attempting to list dogs and pedigrees from as early as 1840, but coat types and sizes were not recorded.

records up to the end of 1901. Ilgner's book is a complete study of the breed and is beautifully illustrated. The next major work, as far as I know, was *Mit Dem Dachshund Unter Der Erde* written by Hugo Siegwart – a very impressive book, published around 1910.

THE GERMAN VIEW

Wildfowler (Clement Lewis) writes: "A meeting of the German Dachshund Breeders was held during the Hanover International dog show, 21-25/5/1879 and resolutions were agreed, as to points by which Dachshunds should be judged – these were published in *Der Hund*. I now come to the points of Dachshunds as agreed upon by the meeting":

N.B. These were, of course, all Smooths at this time.

1. **General appearance, low and very long structure, deep and well developed chest, legs very short, the fore legs turned inward at the knees, with the feet considerably bent out. The whole appearance is weasel-like. The tail is not much crooked, and is carried either straight up or a little sloping. Hair close, short and smooth, expression intelligent, attentive and lively. Weight not over 10 kilos.**
2. **Head long and pointed towards the nose, forehead broad and flat, nose narrow, the lips hang over a little, and**

form a sort of fold in the corner of the mouth.
3. Ears of medium length, tolerably broad and round at the ends, placed high up, and at the back of head, so that the space between eye and ear appears considerably larger than with other hunting dogs; they are smooth and close, and droop with any shaking of the head.
4. Eyes not too large, round and clear, rather protruding, and very sharp in expression.
5. Neck long, flexible, broad and strong.
6. Back very long, and broad in the hind parts.
7. Breast broad, ribs deep and very long, and back part of body higher than the front.

SIGNIFICANT IMPORTS

Gernot com Ludenbuhl: An early import from Germany.

Hannemann-Erdmannshiem, pictured in 1896.

8. Tail of medium length, strong at the root, and gradually running to a short point, almost straight, occasionally with a small curve.

9. Fore parts much stronger than the hind, muscular shoulders, which are short, forequarters very short and strong, bending outwards, the knee inwards, and the feet again outwards.

10. Hind legs – knuckles strong and muscular, pasterns very short and quite straight in comparison with the front legs.

11. Fore feet much stronger than the hind feet, broad and the toes well closed; the nails strong, uneven, and particularly of a black colour, with a strong pad to the feet. The hind feet are smaller and rounder, the toes and nails shorter and straighter.

12. Hair short, close, and glossy, smooth and elastic, very short and fine on the ears, coarser and longer on the lower part of the tail. The hair on the lower part of the body is also coarser.

13. Colour black, with tan on the head, neck, breast, legs, and under the tail. Besides dark brown, golden brown, and hare grey, with darker stripes on the back; as also ash grey and silver grey, with darker patches (*Tiger dachs*). The darker colours are mostly mixed with tan and with the lighter colours; the nails ought to be black, and the eyes dark. White is only to be admitted in the shape of a stripe on the chest straight down.

14. Teeth upper and lower meet exactly, they must be strong in every respect.

Those dogs may be considered as faulty which have a compressed or conical head, if the nose is too short or too narrow, if the lips are too long, long faltering ears, thin neck and narrow chest, if the front legs are not regularly bent or if the crookedness of the legs is so strong as not to carry the weight of the body. Further, the feet if they are not regularly formed, if the hind legs are too long, and likewise the tail when too long and heavy and conspicuously crooked. With regard to colour, it is to be said that white as ground colour is also to be considered faulty, with the exception of what is mentioned before.

EARLY WINNERS

Queen Victoria's husband, Prince Albert, is credited with bringing the Smooth-haired Dachshund to the UK in around 1840 but, as Princess Victoria, she most certainly had the breed in 1833. "I dressed dear, sweet little Dash for the second time after dinner, in a scarlet jacket and trousers."

The first prize winners recorded were Mr Corbet's Carl and the bitch Grete, bred by Count Knyphauser of Hanover. Both won special prizes at the great Birmingham show in 1866, the same year they were born. Satan, imported from Stuttgart by Mr Forbes, gained a prize in "an extra class for any known breeds of Foreign Sporting Dogs"; this was at the Birmingham show in 1869.

The next Dachshund shown in the UK was bred by H.R.H. Prince Charles of Saxe Weimar and imported by Mr Fisher. This was *Feldmann*, who was shown at the Birmingham shows of 1870/1/2, and at Edinburgh in 1871. He was shown as "a pure German Badger Hound" in the extra class for any known breeds of Foreign Sporting Dogs. At the Birmingham show in 1872, he was beaten into second by the Earl of Onslow's Waldman, bred from the Grand Ducal Strain, Darmstadt, Germany. Waldman also won a prize at the Crystal Palace 1872 show. Altogether, Feldmann was the winner of 34 prizes. These shows pre-dated the Kennel Club's organised events. In total, 12 Dachshunds or German Badger Hounds were shown and entered in the first KC studbook of 1873.

Many of our early Dachshunds were also shown with great success on the Continent, including Wagtail, who was awarded the Prix d'honnour for Best Dachshund in all classes at the Brussels show 1885, and Pterodactyl, winner at Spa, Belgium, in 1891. Ch. Pterodactyl was the sire of the two Champion sisters, Belle Blonde and Primula.

THE FIRST CHAMPIONS

The early Champions did not gain their titles as we do today and many different systems were in place before the award was settled in 1904 to winning the three Challenge Certificates that we need today. Prior to 1877, Champion classes were provided at shows for various breeds, but there did not appear to be any definite regulations until 1880. Then, four prizes were needed, one of which had to be won from a Champion class (an extra prize for the best of two or more classes). As far as the records show, Ch. Xaverl was the first dog to gain his title in 1879 by winning the Champion class at the Alexandra Palace show. He was owned by Mr William Arkwright, the great Pointer expert who did so much for both Dachshunds and Pointers. Xaverl was a red Smooth, bred in the royal kennels near Stuttgart in 1876. As far as I can ascertain, he was closely followed by Ch. Dessauer, who was born in 1874. He looks to have been bought and sold at least four times throughout his show career.

Ch. Firs Cruiser: One of the first British Champions, bred from imported German stock.

Ch. Jackdaw, born in 1886.

An example of one of the first Long-haired Dachshunds.

The first class of Dachshunds in the UK was scheduled at the first Kennel Club show at Crystal Palace held from June 17-20th 1873.

Entry 12
1st Mr Chapell Hodge.
ERDMANN age 1 yr
breeder/owner.
Sire: the late Henry Treaby Esq's dog
Dam: owner's Waldine (Imported from Germany) .... sale price £10 10s 0d

2nd Rev. G Lovell's. **SATAN** not for sale
Extra prize Hon. Gerald Lascelles. **SCHNAPS** age 5 yrs
Breeder Viscount Lascelles
Sire: Peter
Dam: Undine
sale price £100

VHC Mr David Elphinstone Seton's **DACLIS** age about 2

yrs. (Imported from Konigsberg)... not for sale

VHC The Earl of Onslow's **WALDMANN** age 3 yrs
sale price £1000

The most astonishing entry was of 3 pups aged 1 month, obviously brought to the show so their dam *Juliet* (also entered) could feed them during the show!

Waldmann was a very important sire and three of the early exhibitors, The Earl of Onslow, the Rev. Lovell, and the Hon. Gerald Lascelles, played an important part developing the breed in the UK.

THE LONG-HAIRED DACHSHUND
Mrs Allingham is considered by most to be the pioneer of the Long-haired Dachshund. At the turn of the 20th century she had

a kennel of Longs, based on Austrian stock. This was maintained until the outbreak of the First World War in 1914. She did not show her hounds, so the variety was mostly unknown in the UK until the early 1920s when a brace was brought back from Germany for Dr Fitch Daglish – namely, **Ratzmann vom Habichtshof** and **German Champion Gretel 3rd von Lechtal**.

Ratzmann was shown at Crufts in 1922 and caused a big stir, when gaining the dog Challenge Certificate over the entire entry of top-winning Smooths at that time. After a somewhat shaky start, with a fair amount of in-breeding due to the lack of Longs available, and with further imports, the breed took off. The Long-haired club was formed in 1929.

Dr Fitch Daglish did not consider the variety had any sort

Woolsack: He was the first Wire-haired Dachshund to be shown in the UK.

of spaniel blood in the genes, but I think it is fair to comment that the early pictures show a very spaniel-like type, with longer legs and typical low-set spaniel ears, which can still be seen to this day.

THE WIRE-HAIRED DACHSHUND

F. Jester's book on hunting was printed between 1797-1808. This has the very first record I can trace of a Wire-haired Dachshund. They were not very popular and did not make any real headway, according to Major Ilgner, until the German Teckel Klub was formed in 1888. **Mordax** was one of the very first German Wires shown, at the Berlin show in 1888. He had a good outline, and although his coat was thought too soft, he won the prize "which was well deserved". To me, he looked as if he could have benefited from a

good strip out! In those days there was often a throwback to the rough-haired Pinscher, from which the early Wires had sprung.

English horse dealers, who were often on the continent looking for bargains, came back to Germany with various terriers to mate to the Smooth-haired Dachshund, the most successful cross being that which included the Dandie Dinmont. Major Ilgner came by the influential Waldo in 1883, and another special sire was Mentor-Ditmarsia, to whom all our British hounds can be traced.

The first Wire-haired Dachshund to be shown in the UK, was **Woolsack**, born in 1888 and imported from Baron von Gemming. He looked a strong, black-and-tan dog of fair type. The breed carried on in a small way, but the First World War seemed to put an end to all

interest in the variety. In 1927 a consortium of 15 potential Wire-haired breeders got together to form the Wire-haired Dachshund Club. The first imports came over from Germany the same year.

One of these imports became the first Champion in the breed: **Frizle von Paulinenberg**. Wires have since gone on from strength to strength, with the Miniature Wire – which occurred in the occasional litter– not being taken up until the late 1950s. They were the last of the six varieties to be recognised. **Kiwi of Dunkerque**, a small Standard, may be said to be the mainstay of the variety. Owned by Sir Charles Lambe, he mated her to a Mini Smooth, with good results. Also, of course, there were several imports from Germany. Mrs Molony's Huntersbroad kennel was based on German stock, including the famous **Aggi – Schmitz**. As so many had been bred down from the Standards, the weight limit was allowed to be 12 lbs (5.4 kgs) until the mid 1960s, which helped the breed develop. The first Champion, when CCs were granted in 1959, was **Jane of Sillwood**, made up in that year, followed by the first dog Champion, **Coobeg Ballyteckel Walt Weevil**, in 1960.

MINIATURE DACHSHUNDS

Early Miniatures no doubt turned up mainly as "runts" in the litters around the turn of the century, and the smaller size (which was named Kaninchen) was felt to be very useful in dealing with smaller game, such as rats and rabbits. The small Standards (Zwerg) were also useful in tackling the smaller foxes and holding them until they could be dug out. They were deliberately bred to small toy-type terriers or small pinschers. This gave many of these Miniatures round skulls, staring goggle-eyes, longer legs and less angulation, and it has taken many years of dedicated work to breed these faults out of the Miniature.

In 1925/6 the Danish Miniature Smooth, **Hans von Fehmarn**, and the bitch, **Bitterlin**, imported by Miss New and Lady Blakiston, made their impact in this country. They retained a bitch from this pair, with another going to Mrs Howard of the famous Seale kennel. From these and other imports a steady stream of good-quality little ones were shown and bred from. Mrs Howard reckoned

Ch. Marcus of Mornyvarna: The first Miniature Long-haired Dachshund Champion.

that the little dog **Kleincurio**, who had been born in quarantine and given to her, was "an absolute goldmine". He weighed just 6 ½ lbs when fully grown. Mated to small Standards, he produced many fine Miniatures and his name is behind all the early good dogs of this variety.

Similarly, the first good Mini Longs were imports from Germany. These had been bred with drop-eared Papillon-crosses to help bring the size down, but it took many years of hard work before the Papillon type was bred out. The mainstay in the pedigrees of all Mini Longs was **Halodri von Fleezensee**. Some of the best for type were bred down from the small Standards that occasionally turned up in the litters at that time.

The Miniature Dachshund Club was formed in 1935 and continues to this day to look after the three Miniature varieties. In 1937 a Standard of Points was prepared, to include the important clause that the weight limit for the tinies should not exceed 11 lbs (5 kgs). In fact, the breed was then divided into:

Heavy-weights, not exceeding 25 lbs; Medium-weights not less than 18 lbs or over 21 lbs; Light-weights not less than 13 lbs or over 17 lbs and the Miniatures.

BREED STATUS

By 1949 separate breed status was given to the Long and Smooth varieties; the first Champion of either variety was Portman-Graham's Long-hair, **Marcus of Mornyvarna**. He was originally registered as a Standard, but when Minis were given separate registrations he was transferred to the new register. The Mini Wires followed later on with Championship status, granted in 1958 and, with their extra weight advantage, were able to make good progress in a relatively short period of time.

The breed with all its six varieties and sizes has gone from strength to strength from these early days and at the current time totals over a third of the Kennel Club's Hound Group registrations in the UK.

INFLUENTIAL DACHSHUNDS

Dachshunds of all coats have always been very fortunate to have formidable or awe-inspiring breeders with great knowledge of dogs in general and construction in particular, in their midst. These clever breeders and exhibitors, some current and some long departed, leave a legacy for others to follow.

Many breeders of dogs feel it *infra dig* to campaign an exhibit past its title. This is not the case in Dachshunds; all six varieties

Ch. Bronia Conquistador: A breed recordholder with 51 CCs and a sire of many Champions. Owned by Fran Mitchell.
Photo: Carol Ann Johnson.

Ch. Swansford Arraandor: Best in Show winner, owned by Daniel Roberts.
Photo: Diane Pearce.

have turned up multiple CC winners over the years, and all six varieties have won All Breeds Best in Shows at Championship level.

LONG-HAIRS

In Long-hairs, sire supreme is Ch. Bronia Conquistador who, to date, has sired 19 Champions with, perhaps, more to come, thanks to frozen semen. Not just a good sire, this boy won 51 CCs to become the breed recordholder, plus 12 Hound Groups and two All Breed Best in Shows. Quite a record.

At the time he was competing with yet another superstar, Ch Swansford Arrandor, himself a Best in Show winner and the recipient of 49 CCs, making him the previous recordholder, which, in turn, he took from Ch. Kennhaven Caesar, who won 44 CCs. Caesar was sired by Champion Imber Coffee Bean, who was the sire of 15 Champions, making him the previous top Long-haired sire.

In Long-haired bitches, Ch. Frankanwen Gold Braid won 40 CCs with 13 Hound Groups and two All Breed Best in Shows. She

Ch. Southclff Starsky: Top male Miniature Longhaired.

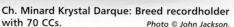

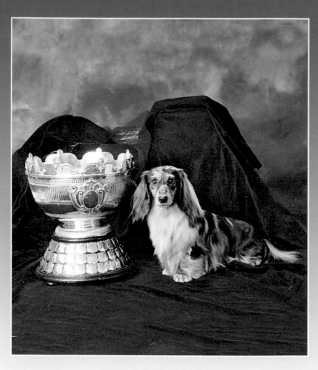

Ch. Minard Krystal Darque: Breed recordholder with 70 CCs. *Photo © John Jackson.*

Ch. Wildstar Wremember Me: Former bitch breed recordholder. *Photo © Roy Wood.*

took this record from Ch. Rebecca Celeste of Albaney, who won 30 CCs. Gold Braid was also the dam of six Champions, so obviously not just a pretty face. Seven Long-hairs have won All Breeds Best in Shows.

MINI-LONGS

Miniature Longs have for many years been the most popular of the six varieties, according to show entries and registrations, so great credit goes to Ch. Sierry Lord of The Ring, who won 11 CCs and a myriad of Reserves,

and sired 16 Champions to make him leading sire.

Ch. Southcliff Starsky was one-time CC recordholder and still is top male, but reigning supreme is Ch. Minard Krystal Darque, who has amassed 70 CCs and is also a Group winner. Previously, the bitch recordholder was Ch. Wildstar Wremember Me, who took it from Ch. Delphic Debrett.

The first and only All Breed Best in Show winner of this variety is Ch. Woodheath Silver Lady, who won at WELKS in 1990.

SMOOTHS

Smooth Dachshunds were considered to be the blueprint for the breed; therefore, I feel it fitting that this variety produced not only the top sire in Smooths but also the top Dachshund sire of all varieties. Ch. Silvae Sailors Quest was born in June of 1946 and won 10 CCs in the stiffest competition. As a sire he was formidable, siring 22 Champions and eight CC winners. This is even more remarkable when it is remembered that he was dead

**Ch. Rhinefield Amala:
Breed record holder in
Smooths with 52 CCs.**
Photo © Len Mitchell.

**Ch. Pipersvale Pina
Colada: the first Miniature
to win Best in Show,
owned by Betty Munt.**
Photo: Anne Roslin Williams.

before his fifth birthday. We can only imagine what his tally could have been had he had a normal lifespan.

Many Smooths were very prolific winners. Ch. Turlshill Troubador winning 50 CCs, taking over from Champion Rhinefields Diplomat and then Champion Rhinefields Amala; beating them all to become the recordholder with 52 CCs to her credit. Over the years, 11 Smooths have won All Breeds Best in Shows at Championship level.

MINI SMOOTHS

In Miniature Smooths again, as in Longs, the top dog is also the leading sire, this being Ch. Pipersvale Pina Colada. He had the distinction of being the first Miniature of any coat to win an All Breeds Best in Show. This he did at Southern Counties in 1983. His tally of CCs was 71, making him the top-winning Dachshund of all time. As a sire, his total was 23 different CC winners. Clever boy!

Ch. D'Arisca Delicacy produced five CC winners, but

Ch. Luxonfield Black Magic of Wimoway was the dam of five Champions.

After the Best in Show win of Pina Colada, his kennelmate, Ch. Jarac Chocolate Surprise at Pipersvale, did the same at Midland Counties in 1990, and a third Best in Show winner for the variety was Champion D'Arisca Candice at Driffield in 1996.

Several lovely bitches in this variety won multiple CCs, many competing against each other, making for high-quality competition. The winner is Ch.

Mordax - an early Wirehaired Dachshund.

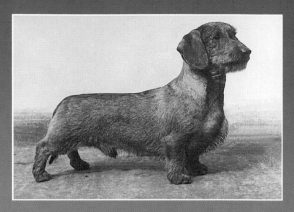

Ch. Gisbourne Inca: Winner of five all breed Best in Show awards. *Photo © Anne Roslin Williams.*

Ch. Drakesleat Klunk Klick of Andyc: The leading male in Mini Wires.

Ch. Lankelly Bryony: Top winning Wire bitch, owned by Pamela Poulter. *Photo: Alan V. Walker.*

Ch. Drakesleat Ai Jinks: Breed recordholder with 33 CCs, owned and bred by Zena Thorn Andrews.

Photo: Sally Ann Thompson.

Siouxline Angelina, who won 24 CCs; she was also a Group winner and multiple Group placer.

WIRE-HAIRS
Wire-hairs took the show world by storm in the early 1960s. When Ch. Gisbourne Inca came out, he won five All Breed Best in Shows and more CCs than any other dog of any breed. This record stood for many years until eclipsed by the Chow Chow Ch. Ukwong King Solomon, who in turn was overtaken by the American Cocker Spaniel Sh. Ch. Homesteads Tiffany With Boduf. To my knowledge, this record still stands.

Inca's kennelmate, Ch. Krystona Augustus, amassed the breed record with 66 CCs and Ch. Andlouis Black Knight won 54. What fierce competition in this variety!

In bitches, Ch. Lankelly Black Bryony is queen with 40 CCs and she also is a Group winner and multiple Group placer.

In the league of top sires, Ch. Gisbourne Inca and his other kennelmate, Ch. Mordax Music Master, are supreme, overtaking each other's tally on occasions, but as Inca was siring Champions for 10 years, I think it's fair to say he wins.

MINI WIRES
Miniature Wires are a clean sweep for one kennel. The leading CC-winning male is Ch. Drakesleat Klunk Klick of Andyc with 27 CCs. Top Bitch and recordholder is Ch. Drakesleat Ai

Jinks, who won 33 CCs, and the leading sire of the breed is Ch. Drakesleat Ris Otto, who sired 14 Champions. In bitches, Top Brood is Ch. Drakesleat Fairy Nuff, dam of six Champions. The only General Championship Show Best in Show for the variety was won by Ch./Jap. Ch. Drakesleat Just Dis Once at Darlington in 2006. What a record...

THE DACHSHUND IN AMERICA

Interestingly, Dachshunds seem to have appeared on the scene in the United States around the same time as in Germany and England. According to AKC records, Dachshunds were recognised as a breed in 1885 and the Dachshund Club of America became a member club of the AKC in 1895.

The history of the Dachshund in the United States is a checkered one in regard to breeding and popularity. Early breeding programmes appeared to be concerned primarily with importations from Europe, particularly Germany and England. However, over the years, serious breeders in the United States developed sound breeding plans and many fine individuals and lines resulted. In looking specifically at how the Dachshund developed in the United States, we must look to certain individuals who dedicated themselves to producing Dachshunds that embodied the qualities that made them fine examples of the breed.

Am. Ch. Favorite von Marienlust: This Dachshund had a profound influence on the breed in the USA.

Am. Can. Ch. Hundelben HoMar Aquarius, owned by Christine Taylor. *Kathy Garcia Photos.*

THE VON MARIENLUST LINE
In the late 1930s, the kennel name von Marienlust appeared on the scene. This was a defining moment in the development of the Dachshund in the 20th century, particularly for Smooths. The von Marienlust kennel was established by Josef and Maria Mehrer, and their line produced many top-winning dogs, as well as many outstanding producers. The pedigrees of many present-day Dachshunds are likely to contain the name von Marienlust.

The list of outstanding dogs bred by the Mehrers is a lengthy and admirable one, but one name stands out among the others... Ch. Favorite von Marienlust. Favorite's prowess as a producer warrants him a place of honour in the annals of Dachshund history. For it was Favorite, along with other von Marienlust dogs, who appear to have set the consistency of type for the Dachshund as we know it today.

The von Marienlust line had a profound influence on the overall appearance of the Dachshund. Pictures taken in the 1800s and the early 1900s show the Dachshund with longer, crooked legs, feet turned outward, a shallow chest, and a curved topline. The Mehrers, along with other serious breeders at that time, did much to produce a dog lower in leg, with a deeper chest, straighter legs and feet, and a level topline.

LONG-HAIRED DACHSHUNDS
Many kennels and individuals were instrumental in the development of the Long-hair in the United States, but one name that invariably emerges in any discussion of Long-hairs is that of Mary Howell and her Bayard kennel. Mary Howell's well-thought-out breeding programme produced Long-hairs that had a consistency of type and structure. She has been quoted as saying that type is not just a word but a concept of all that is correct.

The Bayard Long-hairs had beautiful heads, correct fronts, and long ribbing – all desirable qualities in a good Dachshund. No particular individual dog stands out as the one who had the most profound influence on the Long-hair type that the Bayard kennel produced, but rather it was the combination of excellent dogs in Bayard's breeding programme that consistently produced and set the type for the Long-hairs that we see today.

WIRE-HAIRED DACHSHUNDS

Two names surface when looking to a particular dog or dogs who had a strong influence on present-day Wire-hairs: Ch. Vantebe's Draht Timothy and Ch. Pondwick's Hobgoblin.

Peggy Westphal, whose kennel name was Westphalen, owned Timothy. Timothy had a correct, harsh wire coat, possessed substance with elegance, and was lower-stationed than most of the Wires of his time.

Nancy Onthank, whose Rose Farm kennel was well known, brought Ch. Pondwick's Hobgoblin from England to the United States. Hobgoblin also brought to Wires a harsh coat, overall good balance, a sturdy, yet elegant presence and he too was set lower than most of the Wires of his time.

Each of these individuals made significant contributions to establishing a more consistent and desirable Wire type. Combining the bloodlines from both of them proved to be quite

Midnight Token of Love, owned by James Hall.   *Photo: David Sombach Photography.*

successful. This combination was instrumental in establishing the Wire type that is seen today.

MINIATURES

Miniatures were imported to the United States around 1930. The first ones exhibited in the United States were shown at the Dachshund Club of America Specialty Show in 1934. It is difficult to name any one breeder or any specific dogs that can be credited with establishing the Miniature as we know him today. There were many dedicated Miniature breeders in all parts of the country who worked tirelessly to produce quality Miniature Dachshunds. Some kennel names that are associated with early

breeding programmes that advanced Miniatures are De Sangpur, Tubac, May's, Garner's, and Webb's.

Miniatures began to come into their own during the 1960s and 1970s. Since then, they have evolved into the lovely Miniatures of consistent quality that we see today.

INFLUENTIAL BREEDERS

Dachshund breeders who have been influential in the development of present-day Dachshunds in the United States would comprise a list far too long to be presented here. Thus, just a few of them from each coat variety and size will be mentioned:

- **Smooths:** Polly Fleming (Fleming's), Kaye Ladd (Laddland), Joyce Warren (Joy-Den), Janine Sudinski (Lucene's).
- **Long-hairs:** Walter and Mary Jones (Walmar), Dan Harrison (Boonedox), Paula Carter (Solo's), Hannelore Heller (Han-Jo's).
- **Wire-hairs:** Liz Heywood (Starbarrack), Sharon Johnson (J's), Shirley Ray (Raydachs), Frederick and Carol Vogel (Brodney Schoolhouse).
- **Miniatures:** Susan Jones (Sleepytime), Cliff Simeones and Robbie Addison (Add-Sims), Blanche Schoning (Scoshire), Jeff and Karyn Dionne (Wagsmore).

Ch. Treis Pinheiros Starbarrack Kent, owned by Liz Heywood. *Photo: Perry Phillips.*

WORLDWIDE INFLUENCE

While it is clear that the Dachshund originated on the Continent and was brought to the UK by early enthusiasts, today there are Dachshund lovers around the world who want them as pets, for showing or as working dogs. Although there has always been some export of UK dogs abroad, over the past few years there has been a greater introduction of overseas bloodlines into the UK stock, partly due to the easing of the quarantine restrictions here and also the use of imported semen.

The introduction of overseas bloodlines, carried out by knowledgeable breeders, into our varieties in the UK has not only extended the gene pool, but has complemented our bloodlines. As long as the relevant health and DNA testing is done for both imports and exports, it should go on enhancing all the varieties of Dachshund across the world.

AUSTRALIA

Australian Dachshunds are mostly based on their own bloodlines with some importation of UK and American stock. The Standards are similar in size to ours, but the Miniatures are far larger, as they are not weighed at shows. In order to try to keep their size down, some Miniature breeders have introduced UK Miniature stock because our dogs are more uniform in size, partly because of our emphasis on the 11lb (5kg) ideal maximum weight.

SOUTH AFRICA

All varieties in South Africa have a small gene pool, and where the breeders once looked to the UK for their new bloodlines, they are now importing from Europe, America, Australia, Malaysia, Canada and New Zealand.

JAPAN

The popularity of the Dachshund in Japan may come as a surprise. In 2003, 171,000 Dachshunds were registered at the Japan KC; they were the most popular breed, representing some 30 per cent of all dogs registered that year. By 2009, Dachshunds had dropped to number three, with 66,000 registrations (versus 5,000 in the UK) which still makes them hugely popular, particularly the Miniature Long-haired variety.

EUROPE

European dogs are mostly based on German lines and it is fair to

A Best in Show line-up in Serbia: BIS winner Int. Ch. Drakesleat Humphrey Gocart.

say that their type varies more than ours, with longer legs and less depth of body, which is what the FCI Breed Standard calls for. It is a similar picture in Scandinavia, where the Wire varieties are extremely popular.

In Europe and Scandinavia working skills are an essential element of the show scene, and this has undoubtedly helped keep their dogs truly "fit for function". There are some great dogs, especially in both the Wire varieties where type is becoming more uniform, and these would achieve high awards in the show ring in the UK as well as in Europe and further afield.

So, while many people would still associate the Dachshund with its country of origin, Germany, it's true to say that the Dachshund is much loved and admired worldwide.

A DACHSHUND FOR YOUR LIFESTYLE

Chapter 3

Unsurprisingly, you are attracted to the Dachshund – now you must decide if this is the breed that will suit your family and your lifestyle. The advantage of choosing a pedigree dog is that you can obtain plenty of information about the look and temperament of the breed. In due course, you will also be guided by a reliable breeder who will have taken time and thought to breed a healthy and well-cared-for puppy that is typical of the breed. Of course, there is nothing wrong with taking on a crossbreed but you cannot really be sure of the look, temperament and size such a dog will grow to, and whether he will be right for you.

Remember, your dog is not a commodity that can be put away for a few days when not required. He will need to be loved and cared for, as he will become a very important part of your family. In the case of a Dachshund, he will most likely be with you for 12 or more years. All dogs are a long-term commitment and should not be bought on a whim.

THINKING ABOUT YOUR LIFESTYLE

Many breed club secretaries are contacted by prospective buyers who are not suited, at that time, for the ownership of a Dachshund. Mostly, they are out at work all day and expect a dog to be happy when left alone for a considerable period of time. It is best to have it pointed out that a dog in this situation will become lonely, will chew furniture, mess and probably bark a great deal through sheer boredom. It is more than likely that he will become a problem dog and be very difficult to live with.

It is possible to have a well-adjusted dog when working away from home, but arrangements have to be made for someone to come in to the home to take him out for exercise and give him the opportunity to relieve himself. Also, time has to be set aside for exercising and feeding before leaving for work. It is quite understandable that reputable breeders will not sell their puppies to people who have to work away from home every day.

Saying this, it does not mean that a Dachshund should not be left at all. It is important to train him from a puppy to be able to be left alone intermittently for short periods during the day.

SIZE AND COAT

As there are two sizes and three types of coat of Dachshunds, you will have to consider what coat type you are drawn to and also whether you want a Standard or a Miniature. If you are a family household with youngish children

You need to work out whether a Miniature or a Standard is best suited to your lifestyle.

or teenagers, you could probably choose either size. The Standard is a much bigger and stronger dog to control than a Miniature, so if you are older and require a dog that you can pick up easily, then a Miniature would be more suitable than an exuberant Standard. This also applies if you lead a more sedentary life. In this situation, a Miniature would be more acceptable to your lifestyle.

Although both sizes can live quite happily in town or country, the Miniature is perhaps more suited to urban living with its smaller houses and gardens. But as long as your Dachshund is with you, he is very happy. If you intend to take him around with you and your family in the car and also take him on holidays, then size must also be a consideration.

It must be remembered that Dachshunds are hounds and, when fully grown, both sizes require some free running if possible – when they have been trained to be properly controlled,

of course. If it is not possible, then a good run in the countryside or park on an extending lead will go some way to satisfy their hunting instincts as well as keeping them fit and alert. Both Standards and Miniatures enjoy their walks but are adaptable to their owner's way of life; if the weather is inclement, they are just as happy to curl up in front of the fire. It is usually found that once a Dachshund owner, always a Dachshund owner, although there may be an alteration of size over the years, as a Miniature may be more suitable for older people.

The choice of coat is entirely a matter of personal preference. The individual coats and characteristics are explained fully in *Chapter One: Getting to Know Dachshunds*.

EXPENSE
When you are at the point of purchasing a Dachshund, you must take into consideration not just the price of the puppy but the expense involved in the cost of

food, bedding, toys and veterinary attention, which would include paying for worming pills and routine vaccinations. You may also wish to budget for insurance cover. Dachshunds are pretty healthy as a rule, but it is advisable to shop around for the pet insurance deal that best suits you so that if your dog has an accident or becomes ill, the majority of your bills will be covered and you will have peace of mind.

If you are considering purchasing either a Miniature or Standard Wire-haired Dachshund, you should bear in mind that this coat type entails a trip to the grooming parlour about twice a year to be hand-stripped and tidied. You can, however, do this yourself with a little guidance from your breeder who will always be willing to give you help and show you how it should be done.

The other financial consideration is what to do about holidays. If you intend taking your

Dachshund with you on holiday, there is probably little or no extra expense and he will enjoy the whole experience in your company. Unfortunately, it is not always convenient or practical to do this, so you must consider the cost of either having a dog-sitter to live in and look after your pets at home, or set about finding a reliable kennel. If you intend leaving your Dachshund in kennels, the sooner your young dog gets used to the kennel the better. Perhaps you should let him go in for a day or a weekend so he becomes used to the experience.

Visit a few boarding kennels before deciding on one, and, if you have any doubts, do not leave him there – go on looking.

It is a bonus if you can take your Dachshund on holiday; if you need to make other arrangements, it can prove expensive. *Photo: Sally Ann Thompson.*

MALE OR FEMALE?

Both sexes of Dachshund are loving and loyal in their disposition. Many people say that females are more loving than males, but male Dachshunds, whatever the size, can be just as affectionate and eager to please their owner. Some females can be a little moody before, during and after their season. When a bitch comes into season, which is usually every six to nine months, although it can be longer, it lasts for about three weeks during which time you have to make sure she does not come into contact with interested males.

Generally, temperament is down to each individual dog and how he is reared and trained. If there is no special reason for choosing a female as opposed to a male, go to see the puppies with an open

mind and speak to the breeder, who knows the temperament of their breeding and also what personality is showing through in the litter of puppies.

MORE THAN ONE?

If you are considering having more than one Dachshund to join your family, the consensus of opinion is not to choose two puppies of the same sex, from the same litter. Some puppies of the same litter get along fine together for a while – sometimes for ever – but there is a possibility you may encounter problems with them as they mature. They can start to be argumentative and this could escalate to a serious fight. Once this has happened, it may lead to on-going conflict between them, which could lead to long-term problems.

If you want two Dachshunds, it is probably advisable to wait for approximately 12 to 18 months before you bring home the second dog. If there is going to be trouble, it is between the same sexes, so ideally the second Dachshund you bring in should be the opposite sex to the one you own. Then it is advisable that you either have the male castrated or the female spayed to stop you having problems every time the female comes into season.

Of course, there are always exceptions to the rule and you may be able to own two Dachshunds of the same sex very happily for all their lives – but it is better to know what can happen before a problem arises and you find that you have to rehome one of your dogs for their sake as well as yours.

If you take on an older dog, you will need to help him to settle into his new home.

TAKING ON AN OLDER DOG

You may be considering giving a home to an older dog because you will not have to go through the labours of rearing a puppy. Older dogs are sometimes available from a breeder or from Dachshund Rescue. However, you must be prepared to put in just as much time, as older dogs – just like older people – are more set in their ways and it will take time and patience to get the dog to settle into your lifestyle. If you obtain a Dachshund that has lived in kennels, you may have to deal with house-training as well. Think carefully before doing this – but a

successfully rehomed Dachshund can be a great joy. Just do not think it is always easy; a Dachshund settling into a new home needs a lot of love and understanding.

If this is the road you would like to go down, you can contact Dachshund Breed Rescue (see Appendices). This organisation is in the enviable position of having a waiting list for homes available to rescue dogs, so, fortunately, there are not kennels full of Dachshunds waiting for new homes.

Another way of finding an older dog is to contact breeders through the various Dachshund clubs.

Breeders may have an older female available, who has perhaps had a litter and now needs a permanent home, or a male that has been shown and it is felt that it is better for him to move on so that he can have the individual attention from a loving owner rather than being one of a group for the rest of his life.

WHAT ROLE?

If you are looking for a Dachshund puppy primarily as a companion, your aim is to find a healthy dog who will give you a lifetime of affection and friendship. You will place more emphasis on the temperament of the litter than how they adhere to the Breed Standard, but you will still want a good representative of your chosen breed.

If you join one of the many Dachshund clubs, you will find that some of them hold fun days for you and your dog where you can go and meet like-minded people who will love to chat and exchange views about Dachshund ownership.

SHOWING DACHSHUNDS

If you decide that you would like to show your dog, it is best to attend a few Dachshund shows first, to see if you are drawn to any specific line of the variety of Dachshund you have chosen to own. Talk to the exhibitors and breeders, and read and obtain as much information as you can before setting out to buy your puppy.

Contact your national Kennel Club and request a list of all the

Dachshund breed clubs. Once you have done that and established where you will be able to see the Dachshunds exhibited, go to the Breed club shows and obtain a catalogue; this will set out all the dogs' names together with their owners' names and contact details. Introduce yourself to the club secretary and explain you are interested in purchasing a dog with the possibility of showing him and you will be pointed in the direction of breeders that may have puppies for sale that they think will be of show standard.

No experienced breeder, of any breed, will claim to be able to sell you a puppy that is definitely suitable for the show ring. There can be no guarantee, as a lot can alter as the puppy grows older. If you go to a reputable breeder, asking for a Dachshund that you would like to show, they will sell you a puppy "that has show potential".

Most importantly, go to the shows, speak to the breeders, watch and listen, and perhaps attend a Dachshund breed seminar. Research your chosen variety of Dachshund and read the Breed Standard for Dachshunds so you have a good idea what you are looking for in your dog.

FINDING A REPUTABLE BREEDER

Whether you want a puppy purely as a companion or one for showing, the same rules apply. Avoid buying a puppy from newspaper advertisements, newsagent windows or pet shops.

By going down that route you cannot be sure that care has been taken in choosing a suitable stud dog, whether the relevant health checks have been carried out, or whether the breeder has devoted their time and energy to rearing a healthy, well-socialised litter of puppies. Also, be careful about buying from websites and look for the official Dachshund breed club sites where anyone advertising will comply with the club's code of ethics.

Firstly, contact your national Kennel Club and you will be put in touch with breed clubs who will be willing to help you in your quest. Obviously there are organisational differences depending on where you live, but the aim of a Kennel Club is to work for the good of all pedigree dogs and to help the general public, and to assist breed clubs and breeders in producing healthy and sound stock that fits the Breed Standards. The health and welfare of pedigree dogs is their priority.

The Kennel Club will give you details of breed clubs, and they, in turn, will put you in touch with breeders who have puppies or are about to have puppies. Telephone them, chat to them and ask questions. They will also ask you questions to see whether you are a suitable Dachshund owner and have the right lifestyle for a puppy. Many will ask you whether you would like to visit before the puppies are born to see the relatives of the impending litter.

Beware of a breeder that does not ask searching questions and is willing to meet you halfway at a motorway service station. It is imperative that you visit where the litter is born and see the puppies with their mother, regardless of how far you have to travel. You may not always be able to see the father, as the breeder may have used a stud dog that lives many miles away.

Puppies are irresistible, but you need to make searching enquiries before making a final choice.

QUESTIONS TO ASK

Here are some questions you might wish to ask the breeder:

- How long have you been a Dachshund owner?
- How long have you been breeding Dachshunds?
- How many litters do you typically have each year?
- Which breed clubs do you belong to?
- Do you show your Dachshunds?
- What successes have you had in the show ring?
- What are the positive traits of this breed?
- What are the negative traits of this breed?
- What health problems does the breed suffer?
- What is the average life expectancy?
- What endorsements, if any, do you put on the puppy's Kennel Club papers?
- What should I do if I ever need to rehome a dog we have bought from you?
- What written information on diet and rearing do you provide?
- What inoculations, if any, will the puppy have had when we collect him?
- Have the parents or puppies been tested for known hereditary problems?
- What insurance cover, if any, do you provide with the puppy?
- How many of these puppies will you be keeping yourself?
- Will you be showing any of this litter?
- How much grooming do they need?
- How much exercise do your dogs get and how much will my puppy need?

The answers you get should give you a pretty good idea about the breeder and their attitude to owning and breeding Dachshunds. Note that anyone who breeds more than five litters per year should have a breeding licence issued by their local authority.

The breeder will generally ask you the following questions:
- Are you out at work all day?
- If you work part-time, how long will the dog be left alone?
- Have you owned a Dachshund before?
- What other dogs or pets do you have, if any?
- If you have children, how old are they?
- Do you have a garden and is it well fenced?
- Do you live in the town or country, in a flat or a house?
- Why do you want a Dachshund?
- Do you intend to show or breed from your Dachshund?

The more questions the breeder asks, the more caring and responsible they are likely to be. Do not be insulted. You will find that this is the kind of breeder that will be willing to give you guidance all through the dog's life. Their dogs will have had the relevant health checks and they will ensure that the puppies have been socialised by being handled and played with before they go to their new home. Puppies who, for example, have just been left in a shed at the bottom of the garden with very little human contact will find it very difficult to adjust when brought into a home environment.

CHOOSING A PUPPY

In most cases, the breeder will not invite you to see the litter until they are around four weeks old. You should not visit if you have been in contact with an ill dog, as you may carry germs to the unvaccinated puppies.

When you go to choose your puppy, which will be any time from four weeks up to approximately 12 weeks, be guided by your instincts and also by the breeder. Generally, people say that you should not go for a puppy if he hides in a corner, as this shows he is nervous and may lead to problems later. However, experienced breeders who take into account the good temperament, as well as the soundness of a breed, rarely encounter this problem. Some pups in the litter may be quieter and others more outgoing, but they should all be sound and healthy specimens of the breed. The breeder will have watched the puppies closely as they have grown, and will help you to find the pup that is likely to be most suitable for you, your family and your lifestyle.

If you are choosing a Dachshund puppy for the show ring, the breeder will point out those that have the most show potential at this particular time. It is a good idea to take someone along with you who has a good knowledge of Dachshunds and will also be able to guide you to the right puppy for your requirements.

Many breeders will ask for a deposit when you have made your

Watch the pups play together so you can get an idea of their individual personalities.

choice. This will reserve your Dachshund until he has reached eight to 12 weeks old, when he will be able to leave his mother and littermates.

ASSESSING THE LITTER

Hopefully, you will arrive at the breeder's home before the puppies have a meal, as pups tend to sleep after they have eaten. Puppies spend most of their day playing, eating or sleeping, so it is best to try to choose a time when they are at their most active.

Make sure you are happy with the look of where the puppies are kept and reared. The puppy pen or room should be clean and warm without any sickness or diarrhoea lying around. It should be a pleasant and happy environment for the mother and her pups. If you are lucky enough to be going in the summer months, you may find the puppies

enjoying the sunshine and freedom of being outside.

Watch the puppies and see how they interact with their mother and play with each other. The pups should be inquisitive, bold and friendly, although if they are confronted by a number of visitors, they may take a moment or two to adjust to the situation.

Ask the breeder whether you can handle a puppy. When you hold a puppy or an older dog, support him under the chest and abdomen with one hand while steadying the back end with the other hand. The eyes should be bright with no discharge. There should also be no discharge from the nose. Make sure that the puppies do not have any parasites such as fleas or ear mites. Check the ears are clean and free from any discharge or strong smell, as this would indicate the presence of ear mites. The coat should be

The breeder will help you to assess show potential.

In Wire-hairs there are two coat types: the classic wire (left) and the pin-wire (right).

Colour may change as a puppy matures. This puppy is shaded red and will end up the same colour as the adult.

shiny, not dry or scurfy, and the skin should be supple. The body should be well rounded, not thin or pot-bellied, which could indicate worm infestation. Finally, look at the feet and check that the nails have been kept short and not left long and unattended.

SHOW POTENTIAL
When you go to a breeder to purchase a potential show Dachshund you must assess the litter as mentioned earlier, but follow it up by looking at the construction of individual puppies that the breeder guides you towards. If it is at all possible to leave the final decision to between 8 and 12 weeks, it will be much easier for you and the breeder to make the choice, as the puppy will then be more developed.

It is imperative that you assess the puppy's overall construction and balance. You must read and digest the Dachshund Breed Standard before you go.

Look at the head – is it the correct length and shape with correct eye shape and colour? Does the mouth have the correct number of teeth and the correct scissor bite with the top teeth closely overlapping the bottom teeth? An incorrect mouth is a fault and your Dachshund should not be shown or bred from. This is just a guideline, as you will only see the puppy teeth. Sometimes when puppy teeth change to adult teeth the bite can alter to overshot or undershot. Nothing is 100 per cent certain in nature!.

The forechest should be showing but not fully developed. Look at the topline and tail set. Make sure the back is not roached or dipping badly behind the shoulders or the tail set on too high. Feel the shape and length of ribbing. The ribs should not be flat and should be carried well back with a short loin. Are the shoulders at the correct angle with a good length of upper arm? Does he have good rear angulation without being overdone? You are looking for a well-balanced Dachshund puppy both ends.

Movement is difficult to assess accurately at this age, as a puppy will probably be very loose at the elbow, but you will be able to see whether he is cow-hocked or flaps his front feet or does other undesirable things with his legs and feet.

If you are considering a male puppy, it is important that he has two descended testicles. Sometimes these are not evident at eight weeks, but you should be able to feel them if they are there, even if they have not fully descended into the scrotum.

All Dachshund puppies are born with a smooth coat, so when you go to see a litter of Long-coated puppies do not expect to see a lot of feathering on the chest, legs and tail – this will grow quite slowly. The Wires, if they have a good coat, will show very little beard and just a few longer coarse hairs on the body, legs and in between the toes. If the Wire puppies have a "need tidying" type of coat, the body hair will be thicker and there will be much more beard and eyebrows showing – sometimes quite profuse and fluffy in the softer coats. It is often the Wire or Long puppy who looks almost smooth until late in puppyhood that eventually grows the best coat.

Once you have satisfied yourself that your puppy has been well reared by a caring breeder and that the breeder thinks that you will be able to give the puppy a good home, then all that remains to be done is to arrange a day to collect your Dachshund.

HELPLINE

If you have any queries or questions about your puppy or your fully-grown Dachshund, you should contact your breeder in the first instance. They would probably want to keep in touch with you and their offspring to see how they have progressed and developed over the years. If, by any chance, that is not possible, then turn to one of the breed clubs (see Appendices) and they will be only too pleased to assist you with any problem or anything you wish to know about your Dachshund.

LAST THOUGHTS

Taking on a Dachshund, or any dog, is a big decision and should not be taken lightly. A dog should not be bought on a whim, as he will be sharing your life with you for many years. Your Dachshund, whatever size or coat, will take up a good deal of your time and effort, but the rewards are great and, hopefully, there is a long and happy life ahead for both of you – so read on to find out how you can prepare for these forthcoming enjoyable years.

Take time to do your homework so you are confident that you choose the puppy to suit your lifestyle.

THE NEW ARRIVAL

Chapter 4

Y ou have visited the breeder and chosen your puppy – now you have to wait until he is old enough to leave his mother and littermates to come to his new home. Remember, reputable breeders will be unlikely to let you take your puppy home before the age of eight weeks. Miniature Dachshunds are still very small at eight weeks, so you may have to wait until your pup is 10 or 12 weeks before you can collect him. While you are waiting, there are preparations you can make.

HOME AND GARDEN

You need to think about the sort of routine you will want your dog to get into and plan accordingly. It is best to start off the way you mean to continue. During the first few weeks after your pup's arrival, it is probably better for him to spend most of his time in your kitchen on a washable floor surface, rather than allowing him full freedom to roam the house. Inevitably, there will be accidents while he is learning to be house-trained, and inquisitive pups are inclined to chew, so keeping him in a smaller area with fewer temptations in the early days will pay dividends. An unsupervised puppy, with a free run of the house, is asking for trouble; you may end up with chewed possessions and accidents on the carpets. At worst, your puppy could get into serious trouble and injure himself as he explores his new surroundings. It is also easier for a pup to learn to be clean if he is kept in the kitchen, with easy access to the garden.

If your house has steps in and out of the front or back doors, you may need to consider building a ramp or putting smaller steps in place to make it easier for the pup to get in and

out without straining himself. You also need to bear in mind the potential risk to a Dachshund's back if he is allowed to go up and down flights of stairs. Although a very young puppy is unlikely to be able to climb the stairs, once he is older he will certainly be able to do so. Coming down stairs puts a particular strain on a Dachshund's back and really should be avoided. You might wish to put a baby-gate at the bottom of your stairs so that there is no possibility of your Dachshund going up and hurting himself.

Electricity can be a source of danger, as few pups can resist chewing wires. You will need to check that all electrical cables from the television, the computer, and any other appliance are fastened out of reach.

Before collecting your puppy you need to ensure that the

garden is fully secure, paying particular attention to fencing at ground level. Dachshunds are keen diggers, so although you do not need a very high fence to contain your dog, you will need to make sure there are no gaps at the bottom of the fence for him to tunnel under. If you have a pond or swimming pool in your garden, make sure it is securely fenced off to prevent accidental drowning.

Some plants are poisonous to dogs, so do some research before collecting your puppy. It is also advisable to make sure any fertilisers or weed-killers are safe for pets and bear in mind that slug pellets are also highly toxic to dogs.

When allowing your puppy access to the garden, be careful not to leave him out unattended for long periods of time, as this encourages barking, destructive behaviour and digging, and, depending on where you live, there is also the risk of him being stolen from your garden.

EQUIPMENT TO BUY

Part of the fun of preparing for the new arrival is buying all the equipment and toys you will need. Pet supermarkets offer a wide choice and you are really only limited by how much you are prepared to spend!

An inquisitive puppy will explore very nook and cranny of your home and garden.

PUPPY PLAYPEN

During the first few weeks a puppy playpen is a good idea, although you might feel this is an unnecessary expense for a relatively short period of use. It helps confine the pup to a smaller area at night and during the day when you are busy doing other things. You can put a small, plastic basket or cardboard box in the playpen for a bed, and the floor of the pen can be covered in newspaper. Your puppy can be left safely in his pen with a few toys and, as he is unable to be clean at night until about three to four months of age, this will mean that any mess he makes at night is easily cleaned up.

INDOOR CRATE

Once your puppy gets to about three months of age he can be introduced to an indoor crate for short periods during the day. Eventually he can sleep in the crate, which will help him learn to be clean overnight. The crate needs to be large enough for an adult Dachshund to lie stretched out comfortably. For a Miniature Dachshund, the approximate size would be 24 inches long, 18 inches wide (60 x 45 cms), and for a Standard Dachshund, 31 inches long, 21 inches wide (79 x 53 cms). As well as the conventional metal crates, there are now lighter, fabric crates available, too. These are fine for short periods of use, but Dachshunds are notorious chewers and a fabric cage might not survive very long in the jaws of a determined puppy.

The crate is a good aid for house-training, as the pup can be put inside to rest after he has had a play session and been fed. After his rest, he can be let straight out in the garden to be clean, and this helps reinforce his house-training.

A folding crate is also ideal if you are taking your dog to a cottage or hotel on holiday, or to visit friends. It means the dog will have his familiar, safe haven and is prevented from being destructive or dirty through the stress of being left in a strange place. The dog will settle quietly in his crate after being exercised. Cages and crates must be thought of as a safe den or haven for your Dachshund and never used as a form of punishment.

When you are going out, you can put the crate in your car. This will give your dog a safe place to travel, and he will not be able to distract the driver by moving around the car. The interior of the car will stay clean after muddy winter walks and, in the event of an accident, the crate will prevent the dog escaping and potentially being run over.

A puppy will see a crate as his own special den.

pup can use when he is not in his crate. A plastic basket-shaped bed is easily washable, and makes a comfortable bed when lined with fleece bedding. A wicker baskets really is not suitable, as the young pup will be inclined to chew it. Many pet stores sell dog duvets, which are a comfortable alternative to synthetic fleece and can be used without the need for a basket, if necessary. However, due to their size, they can be difficult to fit into the washing machine when you need to clean them.

FOOD AND WATER BOWLS

A heavy ceramic dish is best for water, as the pup cannot easily tip it over or pick it up. You'll probably want one bowl for in the kitchen, or wherever the dog spends most of his time, and one for the garden for when he is playing outside. Water should be freely available at all times.

An easy-to-clean stainless-steel dish is best for his food. Plastic bowls can easily be chewed and are best avoided.

GROOMING EQUIPMENT

For a Smooth Dachshund, all you really need is a chamois leather hound-glove to keep the coat in shining condition. Long- and Wire-haired Dachshunds need regular brushing with a good-

COLLAR AND LEAD

By law, your dog must wear a collar with an identity tag whenever he is out for a walk. Your puppy will, no doubt, grow through several different sizes of collar, so it is best to wait until he has completed his vaccinations before buying a suitable-sized collar. A thin leather or nylon collar, available from most pet shops, is suitable. Don't forget to attach an engraved name-tag with your name, address and telephone number.

You will need a lead, either made of leather or nylon mesh, with a strong, unbreakable clasp. An extendable lead can also be useful for early stages of training

in the park, allowing your pup a bit more freedom while you remain fully in control. This type of lead should never be let out on full extension when you are walking beside a road; you will have no control if your dog decides to chase something, perhaps running into the path of a car.

BEDS AND BEDDING

Synthetic fleece is ideal for lining the base of a crate. It is easy to wash, dries quickly and you will find it is also pretty resistant to chewing by a young puppy – and an older dog.

You may also decide to have a dog bed in the kitchen that your

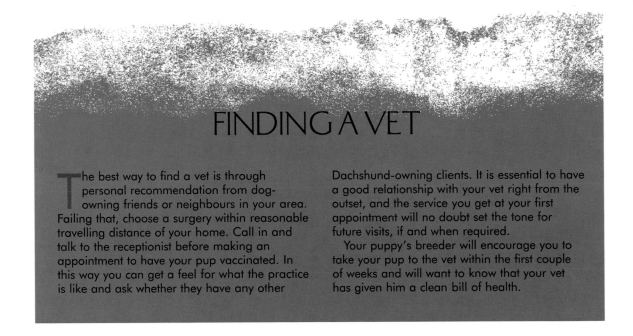

FINDING A VET

The best way to find a vet is through personal recommendation from dog-owning friends or neighbours in your area. Failing that, choose a surgery within reasonable travelling distance of your home. Call in and talk to the receptionist before making an appointment to have your pup vaccinated. In this way you can get a feel for what the practice is like and ask whether they have any other Dachshund-owning clients. It is essential to have a good relationship with your vet right from the outset, and the service you get at your first appointment will no doubt set the tone for future visits, if and when required.

Your puppy's breeder will encourage you to take your pup to the vet within the first couple of weeks and will want to know that your vet has given him a clean bill of health.

quality bristle brush. The feathering on the Longs and furnishings and leg hair on the Wires will need to be combed out with a wide-toothed steel comb. Wires will also need hand-stripping a couple of times a year as adults. You will also need nail clippers or a file, and a toothbrush for all Dachshunds.

TOYS
You can purchase a few toys from your local pet store before collecting your puppy. Soft, squeaky toys should be avoided, as the pup may destroy them in an attempt to get at the source of the squeak. In so doing, he may eat some of the stuffing, which could potentially cause an intestinal blockage and a huge vet bill as a consequence. Plastic and

rubber squeaky toys do not tend to last very long in the teeth of a determined Dachshund– and you do not want to find the remains of the toy but no sign of the 'squeaker'.

Nylon bones and multi-coloured cotton knotted rope toys are more durable and suited to powerful chewers, which even the Miniature Dachshunds can be. Remember: Dachshunds are bred to have strong jaws and teeth. Hide chews are also suitable for young puppies while teething and can also be given to adult Dachshunds under supervision.

CHOOSING A NAME
Although the choice of name for your puppy is very much a personal decision, try to pick a

name that is relatively short and something you will not be embarrassed to call out at a loud volume in your local park!

Because of their mischievous natures most Dachshunds end up with nicknames that suit their characters as well as their 'proper' names, so your initial choice of name is not such a big deal.

COLLECTING YOUR PUPPY
It is important to plan your puppy's homecoming when you will have plenty of spare time to concentrate on meeting his needs – probably not at Christmas, which can be very hectic in many homes. The more time you can invest at the start, the better things will work out for the long-term.

The day finally arrives when it is time to collect your new puppy from the breeder. If possible, arrange to collect your puppy in the morning in order to give him the rest of the day to settle into his new surroundings. The breeder should supply you with:

- A diet sheet
- Information on basic training and breed characteristics
- A record of worming
- A pedigree certificate
- The Kennel Club registration certificate signed on the reverse, ready for transfer of the pup into your ownership
- A sales receipt or contract of sale
- Short-term insurance cover for the first few weeks from when your pup leaves his breeder.

ARRIVING HOME

As soon as you arrive home, take the pup straight out into the garden to give him a chance to relieve himself and to stretch his legs. Bring him into the kitchen and let him explore his new surroundings before feeding him at his scheduled mealtime. Try to resist the temptation of inviting all your family and friends round to meet the new arrival for a couple of days, to allow him a chance to settle in and get used to his new home. Once he is used to his new environment, the more people he can meet in your house, the better. It all helps towards socialising him with people before he has finished his vaccinations and is able to go out and about.

At last the big day arrives, and it is time to collect your puppy.

However, do not allow other dogs to meet him until he has completed his injections.

INTRODUCING CHILDREN

If the puppy is going to live in a house with children, it is essential that the children are taught to respect the puppy and not treat him as an animated stuffed toy. Although it is great fun for children to play with the pup, the play must not become too rough, and very young children should not be allowed to pick the pup up and carry him around. Encourage children to sit on the floor when they are playing with the puppy.

Children (or adults) should never tease or play chasing or pulling games, and the puppy

It is essential to establish mutual respect between a puppy and younger members of the family.

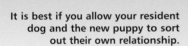

It is best if you allow your resident dog and the new puppy to sort out their own relationship.

must not be allowed to chase or nip. Respectful and caring children can derive great joy from a puppy and vice versa. It can and should be a great relationship.

A small puppy can easily get under your feet, so noisy children running around unsupervised is a recipe for disaster. A puppy can get kicked or trodden on, which would be very distressing for the puppy and not very pleasant for you to have to deal with.

Miniature Dachshunds are tiny as young pups and are therefore vulnerable to injury.

The puppy *must* be allowed to rest in his crate or playpen undisturbed in between play sessions. Never leave children unsupervised while interacting with the puppy.

You will also need to make sure that older children and visitors are shown how to pick up a Dachshund properly. A puppy

needs to be well supported at both the front and the back ends, otherwise you risk hurting his back.

MEETING OTHER PETS
When introducing a new puppy to an older resident dog, plan the first meeting outside in the garden under close supervision, or in a neutral location. The older dog may be frightened of the new arrival or could act aggressively to

start with. Be patient but, above all, never leave them unsupervised until you are sure they are going to get along. They will take a short time to establish a relationship, and the older dog will soon realise that the pup is not a threat.

INTRODUCING THE CRATE

As mentioned before, for the first few weeks the pup will need to be in his playpen at night, but you can still make a start on introducing him to his crate during the daytime. After a play session and a trip outside to relieve himself, put the pup in his crate with a favourite toy. To start with, stay in the room with him and he will soon settle down and sleep. Let him rest for a while and then, when he wakes up, take him straight out to the garden to be clean. He will soon begin to think of his crate as his own special den and will settle down quietly to rest.

ESTABLISHING A ROUTINE

Dogs are creatures of habit and like to have a regular routine, where they know when it is time to eat, to be clean, to sleep and to go for exercise.

MEALTIMES

The breeder should give you a few days' supply of the food your puppy has been eating, together with a diet sheet detailing the quantity he should be fed. Stick to this for the first week or so and, ideally, continue to follow the breeder's advice on feeding. If you wish to change to a different

food, do so gradually over a few days. Start by substituting half the original food with the new food at each meal, then steadily increase the percentage of the new food and decrease the amount of the old food until, after a week, the pup is eating only the new food. In this way, your puppy will not suffer a stomach upset from too rapid a change of food.

There are many good-quality brands of life-stage complete foods suitable for puppies, so it is easy to find one that your pup likes to eat and that keeps him in good condition. There is even small-size kibble designed especially for miniature and toy breeds, which makes feeding Miniature Dachshund puppies easy.

An eight-week-old pup will need four meals a day, and these should be spaced out at regular intervals during the day. Keep to these mealtimes so that your pup gets into a routine. This will also help with his house-training.

For more information on diet, see Chapter Five: The Best of Care.

SLEEPING AND RESTING

Try to establish a settled routine with your new puppy. Remember that pups need a good deal of sleep, so get into the habit of putting the pup in his crate to rest after he has had a play session and a feed, as he will naturally be sleepy at this time.

The breeder will usually give you enough food to tide you over the first few days.

He needs this quiet time to grow and develop. Keep play sessions relatively short when the pup is young – half an hour at a time is more than enough.

For the first few nights, you may find the pup protests when you leave him to go to bed at night. This is perfectly natural, as separation from his mother and siblings can be a stressful experience. You can try leaving a radio on to give him some reassuring sounds. But you should be prepared for some sleepless nights to start with. You will be surprised how much noise a small Dachshund can make and how long he can keep it up. Obviously, if you have close

If you take your puppy outside at regular intervals, he will soon learn what is required.

puppy out to the garden, to an allocated toileting area, at the following times:

- First thing in the morning
- Every time he wakes up
- After each meal
- After a play session
- Last thing at night.

While your puppy is very young and still learning, you should take him out every 15-20 minutes throughout the day. This interval can be gradually lengthened to every half hour as he gets towards three to four months and learns what he is supposed to be doing. He will eventually learn to 'go' on command if you always use the same cue, such as "Busy", every time he performs.

When the pup relieves himself outside, reward him with lavish praise or even a titbit. Dachshunds respond to praise especially well. Simply ignore any accidents made in the house, as scolding your puppy is counterproductive. It will make him fearful, so he is more likely to sneak off and relieve himself out of your sight.

You need to put in a great deal of effort in these early weeks to teach the pup to be clean indoors. It is actually easier to house-train a puppy in the winter months when it is cold outside, as the pup will soon learn that each time he is put outside and he toilets quickly, he gets praised and can come back inside to the warm kitchen as a reward. When house-training a puppy in the summer, the temptation is to

neighbours, this noise is not acceptable. In this instance, it may be necessary for you to move the puppy's crate near to where you are sleeping so he can see you and so you can reassure him or tell him to be quiet in a timely fashion. Ideally, the pup should be tired when he is put to bed, having been fed, played with and toileted first.

HOUSE RULES
In our house, the rules for our dogs are simple:

- Toys are for chewing, not the furniture.
- Barking when someone comes to the door is allowed, but persistent barking for no obvious reason is not.
- Go outside to be clean after waking up and after every meal.
- Sitting on the sofa is by invitation only; otherwise, dogs

sit on the floor.
- Each dog has his own place in the kitchen at feeding time; nobody steals food from another dog's bowl.
- At least one 45-minute walk (for an adult dog) each day.

You will need to decide your own house rules, and this is whatever works for you and your lifestyle. Agree them with all the family and be consistent about applying them.

HOUSE-TRAINING
Dachshunds can be a little more difficult to house-train than some breeds, and Miniatures do typically require more patience than Standards. As with feeding and sleeping, establishing a consistent routine is also very helpful when house-training a puppy.

You will need to take your

leave the back door permanently open and let the pup please himself when he goes outside to be clean. You will then find that when the winter comes and the door has to be shut, the pup will start having accidents, as he has not learnt a proper house-training routine.

GOING OUT AND ABOUT

Until your pup has finished his vaccinations he will need to be confined to exercise in your house and garden. However, that does not mean he cannot be taken out and socialised. Initially you can carry him, as long as he does not mix with other dogs. He can also get used to trips in the car, or to the shops, in his crate. The more varied experiences he can have, as early as possible, the better.

Once your puppy has full immunity at about 12 weeks, and the vet says he can start to go out and about, you can take him for very short walks of five to ten minutes. Try to vary where you take him so that he gets used to walking on pavements with passing traffic and also walking on grass in the local park or nearby countryside. It is vital that you start off-lead exercise and training at this young age while the pup is still immature and focused on his owner, as the hunting instinct is quite strong in some Dachshunds. If your puppy gets used to being off-lead while he is still young and relatively well behaved, it will not have novelty value, so he can be safely let off for essential free-running as an adult.

Early socialisation with people – and with animals – is a vital part of your puppy's education.

For information see Chapter Six: Training and Socialisation.

GROOMING

Right from the start, you should get your puppy used to being handled and groomed. This should be a regular part of his routine, and it is an important aspect of teaching him to be calm when being handled by you, the vet and anyone else.

Start by putting your puppy on a table, where he will be easier to control, preferably on a rubber mat to avoid slipping. If you try to groom him on the floor, he will probably just think it is a game and be harder to restrain. Talk to your puppy calmly and encourage him to stand still while he is brushed gently (if he is a Long or a Wire) or groomed with a hound glove (if he is a Smooth). Longs and Wires also need to have their feathering and furnishings combed out regularly in order to avoid painful knots in the coat.

Once your pup has finished teething at around six months, start to introduce teeth cleaning with a toothbrush and special toothpaste for dogs, which you can obtain from your local pet shop. His mouth will be very sensitive before he has finished teething, so it is best to wait until he has his adult teeth through. Be very gentle when brushing the teeth. Do not forget to brush his back teeth as well as the front ones. There are also some food supplements you can buy to help reduce plaque formation and improve dental hygiene.

Longs and Wires will need the hair round their feet and between their pads trimming regularly to stop mud balling in their feet after walks. Wire Dachshunds will also need their coats hand-

HANDLING AND GROOMING

A puppy needs to be accustomed to being handled and groomed from an early age.

The ears should be examined to ensure they are clean and smell fresh.

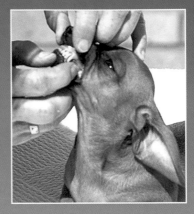

Teach your puppy to open his mouth so you can check teeth and gums.

Lift up each paw in turn.

Stroke along the length of the back.

Gently roll the puppy over on to his back.

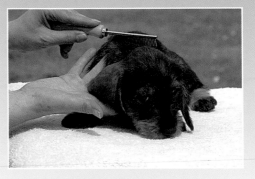

A wire-haired puppy will need to get used to being brushed and combed.

stripping two or three times a year,. A Wire puppy with a typical coat will need the puppy coat stripped off at about four to five months of age to facilitate the growth of the adult coat. This task is best left to a professional dog groomer.

Regular grooming a couple of times a week is essential to maintaining good health. Check the dog's paws, eyes and ears each time, and if you notice any discharge from the eyes, or smelly ears, then see your vet for appropriate treatment.

For more information on grooming, see Chapter Five.

VISITING THE VET

Usually puppies leave the breeder at eight to ten weeks of age, so before you collect your new puppy make contact with a local vet in your area, as the puppy will need to begin his vaccination schedule soon after you bring him home. Make sure you find out if the breeder has already taken him for any injections before you collect him.

At about 12 weeks it is advisable to have your puppy permanently identified by microchip. The vet can do this for you. This unique number on the microchip is recorded on a database so that if your dog goes missing and is later found, he can be returned to you once his microchip is scanned.

WELCOMING AN OLDER/RESCUE DOG

Some people prefer not to have all the intensive training that goes

with taking on a new puppy, or, maybe if they are older, feel they can't cope with the demands of a young dog. An adult Dachshund from rescue or a retired show dog or brood bitch from a breeder is a good alternative in these circumstances.

If you are taking on an adult Dachshund, try to find out as much as you can about his background and the type of lifestyle he has been used to. Maybe the dog is not used to living with children or other pets, so extra care and training would be needed to enable the dog to cope.

When you bring your new adult dog home, it is vital that you act in a calm, consistent manner from the outset. As with a puppy, consistency is the key. Try to establish a routine for feeding and daily walks and grooming sessions. Make an effort to avoid confrontation with the new dog by ignoring bad behaviour and using distractions and rewarding good behaviour with food treats and verbal praise.

It generally takes about a month for an adult dog to settle into a new home and begin to show his true character. Be patient and he will soon adapt to his new environment. If there are any persistent behavioural problems, you may need to seek expert advice and attend training classes with him to help resolve the difficulty. Your vet can advise you on this issue.

FINALLY...

Do not forget to let the breeder know how your puppy is doing after the first few days. The breeder has invested a lot of time and energy in raising your new pet and will want to know that he is settling in with his new family. The breeder will also appreciate photos and progress reports throughout your dog's life.

A responsible breeder will ask that, if you can no longer keep your Dachshund at whatever age, you should let them know and not just pass him on to another home without informing them. Circumstances change, and your dog's breeder may well be able to help find another suitable home.

You will need to give an older dog time and patience to help him settle in a new home.

THE BEST OF CARE

Chapter 5

Over the lifetime of owning a Dachshund, you will become the expert on his care, learning to understand his different moods and his needs. As he grows through puppyhood, matures into adulthood and then develops into a much-loved oldie, you will need to respond with suitable care at each of his life-stages.

You will spend the most time with him. Nobody else – vet, trainer or groomer – will know him as well as you do. While you may take advice from these people, in practice they can only ever see a snapshot of your Dachshund's life and it is up to you to ensure he has the best of care.

If you are a first-time Dachshund owner, your puppy's breeder will invariably be the starting point for information on the breed, and your puppy in particular. Any reputable breeder will be only too happy to provide advice at any stage of your Dachshund's life. However, if you feel you are not getting the information you need, there are numerous Dachshund breed clubs, with experienced officers and committees, who can offer advice and the benefit of many years of experience as Dachshund owners.

To keep your Dachshund fit and healthy, you will need to understand his typical needs for food, exercise and welfare at each of his life-stages.

UNDERSTANDING NUTRITION

In order to understand canine nutrition and what makes for a good, balanced diet, you need to know whether a dog is a carnivore or an omnivore. The modern dog, *Canis familiaris*, is a direct descendent of the grey wolf, *Canis lupus*. All dogs (as well as the cat) are members of the order *Carnivora*, meaning they evolved as carnivores; i.e. they are flesh-eating, predatory members of the animal kingdom.

However, the fact that a dog evolved as a carnivore does not necessarily mean his diet must be restricted to meat; in fact, he is an omnivore. Unlike the domestic cat, which has a relatively short small intestine, dogs can and do digest a wide variety of foods, including vegetables and grains. It is not unusual to see dogs eating grass and they can survive quite happily on a vegetarian diet if that is what you choose for your pet, as long as it contains sufficient protein.

It is not so long ago that the majority of pet dogs would be fed on diets comprising mostly meat and biscuit, together with raw

You need to feed a well-balanced diet that is suited to your Dachshund's age and lifestyle.

- **Carbohydrates:** These include sugars, starches and dietary fibres. They provide some of the energy your dog needs, but many (e.g. cellulose and bran) simply add bulk and act as a filler in commercial dog foods.
- **Vitamins:** Vitamins A, B, D and E take part in a wide range of metabolic activities but are only needed at low concentrations that can be provided as part of any normal, balanced diet.
- **Minerals:** Calcium and phosphorus are essential for strong bones and teeth. Magnesium, sodium and potassium contribute to nerve impulse transmission and muscle contraction. Other minerals are needed in only trace quantities and, like vitamins, are normally present in any well-balanced diet.

One of the big advantages of feeding a commercially produced dog food is that all these essential nutrients will be present in the right proportions and you will not need to add any supplements. In fact, adding supplements could seriously imbalance your dog's diet and lead to health problems.

Most commercial pet foods specify the percentage of protein contained in the diet. Puppies will typically need 28 per cent to provide for their high growth needs. Adult Dachshunds leading the life of a normal pet will need lower levels, around 18-22 per cent as a maintenance diet. Working Dachshunds would require higher levels of protein to meet their needs for additional

bones and any leftovers from their human owner's table. Experienced breeders and owners of kennels of working Dachshunds would instinctively know the right balance of meat and biscuit to feed, along with the appropriate exercise regime, to keep all their hounds in prime condition. Indeed, the few kennels of working Dachshunds (Teckels) today continue to feed a diet of meat and biscuit. That meat might include raw tripe or carcases of fallen farm animals.

However, for most owners of Dachshunds that live in the house and lead the lives of active pets, the multitude of prepared foods from the pet food manufacturers offers a more convenient, and less smelly, option. Clearly, the major pet food manufacturers invest huge amounts of money into

researching the nutritional needs of dogs, but they also invest in manufacturing and packaging methods that make their products easy to store and use in the home environment.

Dogs need the following types of nutrients to survive:
- **Amino acids from proteins:** Dietary protein is made up of essential amino acids and contributes to the energy needed for growth and daily living.
- **Fats and fatty acids:** Dietary fats, which can be derived from animal fats or vegetable seeds, provide the most concentrated source of energy in your dog's diet. Fatty acids help with the absorption of vitamins and are necessary to keep your Dachshund's coat and skin healthy.

energy. You should not feed a high-protein diet to a Dachshund that does not need to burn off high levels of energy. He will simply end up hyperactive and hard to live with.

Pregnant and lactating bitches will need high-protein diets (28 per cent), plus higher levels of dietary fat, to provide for the needs of feeding puppies. An elderly Dachshund, or one whose weight you are trying to control, will need a well-balanced diet that is generally lower in calories, but still has adequate protein and fat, and is higher in fibre.

CHOOSING A DIET

The choice of feeding regime and diet for your Dachshund really boils down to what works best for him, his lifestyle and you.

COMPLETE

Complete foods are easy to manage and simply need to be fed either dry or moistened with a little warm water. Your Dachshund will get a guaranteed balanced diet, with the right nutrients in an easily digestible form. Some pet food manufacturers even formulate Dachshund-specific complete foods. These are designed with the needs of a 'dwarf breed' in mind, and have extra glucosamine, chondroitin and fatty acids to help maintain healthy joints and cartilage. Complete foods vary from flakes to crunchy nuts or shapes. They tend not to smell and are easy to store and keep fresh in sealed bags or airtight containers.

If you have a fussy eater, complete foods can appear to make the situation worse. You may be tempted to supplement the complete food with meat (perhaps mince or chicken), but this will only make your dog more fussy. He will happily scoff the meat and leave the complete food, thus ensuring a totally unbalanced diet.

CANNED

Canned dog meats, fed with biscuit, usually look and smell more appealing both to you and the dog, but you need to ensure you get the right balance of meat to biscuit, so read the manufacturer's instructions carefully. Some Dachshunds can be picky feeders, so you have to be careful that your dog does not simply vacuum up the meat and leave all the biscuit. He then won't be getting the right balance of nutrients.

BARF

The BARF diet is an increasingly popular option. BARF stands for Bones and Raw Food, or Biologically Appropriate Raw Food. It is based on many of the old-fashioned feeding principles, and attempts to mimic the diet of wild dogs, using available raw foodstuffs. A BARF diet will include such ingredients as muscle, meat, bone, fat, offal and vegetable materials.

Fans of the BARF diet claim it results in healthier, cleaner teeth, firmer stools and significantly reduces allergies. It is also likely to be highly palatable for your dog. However, you still have to ensure you are feeding the right quantities and proportions of nutrients.

A complete diet is easy to feed.

Most Dachshunds find canned food very appetising.

There are many advocates for feeding a more natural, raw diet.

FEEDING A PUPPY

Your Dachshund's breeder should give you a few days' supply of the food your puppy has been eating, together with a diet sheet detailing the quantity he should be fed. Stick to this for the first week or so otherwise your puppy is likely to suffer a stomach upset from too rapid a change of food. Each breeder will have their own preference for feeding regimes and for particular manufacturers' brands of dog food. It is wise to be guided by their recommendations initially.

An eight-week-old pup will need four meals a day. A young puppy has a relatively small stomach, so he can only cope with small quantities of food at any one time. It is far better to feed small quantities that your puppy eats completely, and only increase the amount when you are confident that he is going to eat it all without delay. If he starts 'picking' at his food, he is probably being given too much.

Do not leave a bowl of food down if it is not eaten straight away. Pick it up and make your puppy wait until his next planned mealtime. A Dachshund will not starve himself and you need to get him into the routine that you want him to adopt, not one that he chooses. Pandering to his whims, for example by adding

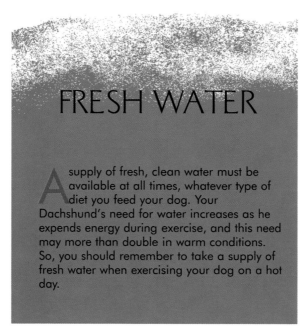

FRESH WATER

A supply of fresh, clean water must be available at all times, whatever type of diet you feed your dog. Your Dachshund's need for water increases as he expends energy during exercise, and this need may more than double in warm conditions. So, you should remember to take a supply of fresh water when exercising your dog on a hot day.

a bit of fresh chicken to a complete food, will quickly teach him that leaving what he does not fancy will be rewarded by something better.

Choose a place to feed your puppy where he will be undisturbed, particularly if you have other dogs (or cats), and stick to this place. It will help to reinforce his eating routine and habits. You will probably have to stand with him to encourage him to stay with his bowl of food until it is completely eaten. Young puppies are inquisitive and have short attention spans, so you may need to keep pointing him back towards his bowl. Do not fall into the trap of making a fuss of him before he has finished his meal, otherwise you will reinforce the habit of 'picking' at food. Dachshunds are generally good

eaters and most will wolf their food down at one sitting. But, if you get into bad habits, you will end up with a fussy eater and those habits are hard to break later on.

In the first few weeks of your Dachshund puppy's life, his mother's milk will have been the main part his diet. However, once he has been fully weaned, and certainly by the time you bring him home, milk is not a necessary part of his diet. Fresh water is all he needs, and, in fact, milk can cause tummy upsets.

Generally, by 12 weeks – maybe a bit later for Minis – you can cut out the evening feed, but the quantity of the remaining three meals must be increased to take account of the pup's growth rate. Keep him on three meals a day until the age of about five months when you can reduce to two feeds daily.

FEEDING AN ADULT DOG

Most people prefer to provide one meal first thing in the morning and one in the late afternoon or early evening. The aim is to feed a quantity that allows your Dachshund to maintain the right weight for his lifestyle – so he's neither underweight nor overweight.

Ideal weight: Your Dachshund is at an ideal weight if you can easily feel his ribs but they are not visible. He should have an obvious waist behind the ribs, when viewed from above. There should be little abdominal fat, and a slight tuck-up should be evident when he is viewed from the side.

Underweight: Your Dachshund is not getting enough to eat if you can easily see his ribs, spine and pelvic bones. You will be unable to feel any fat on his bones, and will possibly notice some loss of muscle mass. He will have an obvious abdominal tuck-up when viewed from the side. In this situation, you should increase the size of his portions and maybe consider finding a food with a higher calorie level.

Overweight: Your Dachshund is overweight if you cannot feel his ribs and can see fat over his back and the base of his tail. He will also have rolls of fat on his neck and over his shoulders. He will have no discernible waist behind the ribs when viewed from above, and you will be able to see excessive abdominal fat or a distended underline, in profile. The risk of obesity increases with age and is more common in neutered animals, and there are associated risks of diabetes and osteoarthritis. The most obvious solution is to reduce the quantities your Dachshund eats – including treats – or move him on to a lower calorie food. His daily exercise should also be increased.

You need to look at your dog – regardless of whether it is a Miniature (right) or a Standard (below) – and work out the correct amount to feed so he does not become overweight.

AVOIDING FUSSY EATERS

This begins with the routine you adopt when you first bring your puppy home. If you fail to get him into a routine of regular mealtimes and expecting him to clean his dish quickly, you run the risk of developing a fussy feeder.

However, most of us have found that Dachshunds are more inclined to be greedy, rather than fussy, so the more common challenge is to keep your dog at an acceptable weight and to avoid any risks of obesity.

A Dachshund is never happier than when he has a chance to use his nose.

A game with a toy provides mental stimulation as well as physical exercise.

EXERCISE REQUIREMENTS

Exercising your Dachshund is as much about giving him mental stimulation as it is about physical exercise. The Breed Standard describes the Dachshund's character as: "Intelligent, lively, courageous to the point of rashness, obedient". A bored Dachshund is likely to be a noisy and destructive Dachshund, so varied daily exercise provides the mental stimulation to keep him happy.

It is important not to over-exercise a puppy. Puppies spend a lot of time sleeping and you need to build up their exercise regime over the first year as follows:

- **12 weeks:** Once your puppy has finished his course of inoculations, take him for a short walk of about five minutes every couple of days or so to help him get used to traffic, other people and dogs.
- **Four months:** Your puppy should be having a 10-minute walk every other day.
- **Five months:** Gradually increase the distance and time to about 15-20 minutes every day.
- **Six months:** He should be going for a 25- to 30-minute walk each day.
- **12 months:** By this stage, you should be giving your dog a 40- to 45-minute walk a day.

Once adult, your Dachshund will take any amount of exercise

AVOIDING BACK PROBLEMS

ntervertebral Disc Disease (IVDD) is the most significant health risk in Dachshunds, and the research indicates that between one in four and one in five Dachshunds will have some degree of disc-related problems in their lifetimes. Dachshunds have a condition known as chondrodystrophy – 'chondro' means cartilage and 'dystrophy' means disorder. This means they are more prone to disc degeneration at an earlier age than many other breeds. The age of incidence for chondrodystrophoid breeds is highest between three and seven years. There is evidence that there is an inherited component to IVDD.

There are several things you can try to do – or not do – to minimise the risk of injury:

- **Regular exercise:** Keep your Dachshund slim and streamlined, as Dachshunds were meant to be. Additional weight can put more stress on the spine.
- **Stairs:** It is essential to limit your Dachshund's use of stairs. Wherever possible, avoid the sudden compressive forces on the spine that result from going down stairs.
- **Jumping:** Be very cautious in allowing your Dachshund to jump on and off furniture, including beds.
- **Ramps:** The use of ramps is strongly recommended, particularly for Standards, including for getting in and out of the back of your car. Minis can be picked up much more easily.
- **Lifting:** When lifting your Dachshund, use two hands, one supporting the chest and one supporting the back.

you care to give. This is equally true of Standard and Miniature Dachshunds. Remember, these were originally working hounds and, when adult, they should still be capable of out-lasting you on any walks.

Too much exercise, too soon, will cause out-turned feet, poor toplines and poor body development. Whether your Dachshund is a pet, a working dog, or a show dog, he must be allowed to grow up naturally, and with exercise suitable for his stage of development. It is far better to allow your puppy to exercise in the garden so he can decide when

he has had enough, rather than taking him on long walks where you risk over-tiring him. Worst of all is an exercise regime of little or nothing during the week, followed by an all-day marathon at the weekend. Your Dachshund will be full of energy until he 'grows up' (if he ever does), but you will have a far fitter dog in the long-term if you do not over-exercise when he is young.

At the end of the day, it is up to you, of course, but do ensure your Dachshund gets out and about so he is well socialised by meeting different people and experiencing different situations. You will

invariably find that, the more exercise you give your Dachshund, the more he will want. He will watch your every move until you pick up his lead, and he will let you know when he thinks it is time to go out for a walk.

Obviously, the type of exercise you give your Dachshund will depend on where you live and what options you have in your local area. He will happily 'pound the streets' if you are limited to walking on pavements. This must *always* be on the lead, however well trained and obedient you think your Dachshund is. Dachshunds have no road sense;

CLEANING EARS

You may need to clean the ears using specially formulated liquid or powder.

Massage the outside of the ear.

Clean with cotton-wool (cotton), making sure you do not probe into the ear canal.

your dog could easily be distracted by a cat or person and try to rush across the road, with potentially fatal consequences.

A Dachshund loves nothing more than exercise in the countryside or a park. Providing it is safe to do so, he can be given free-running exercise and he will enjoy sniffing out all the interesting smells in the hedges and along the tracks. As your Dachshund gets older and becomes a veteran, you will probably find that he slows down and is not quite as keen on the amount of exercise he enjoyed as a youngster. He still needs regular exercise, but tailor it to his slower lifestyle and keep an eye on his weight. If he is getting fat, you either need to reduce his food or increase his exercise, or a combination of both.

GROOMING YOUR DACHSHUND

In the previous chapter, we have described how you should begin to get your new puppy used to being groomed. Regular grooming gives you the opportunity to check your Dachshund for any emerging health or welfare problems. You should be looking out for:

- His overall condition – is he getting too fat or too thin?
- Cuts or scratches that he may have picked up while out walking.
- Small lumps that could be the early signs of a bigger problem.
- Coat and skin condition – is it dry and flaky, or are there any thin or bald patches?

Whether you have a Smooth,

Long or Wire, there are some common grooming tasks you should carry out regularly.

EARS

A Dachshund's ears are not held erect like some other breeds, so they will not necessarily get much fresh air. They can, therefore, become warm, moist areas in which problems can build up. Check that your Dachshund's ears are not smelly and that there are no brown, waxy deposits. If he is shaking his head or scratching constantly, you will probably need to seek veterinary advice, as he may have an infection of ear mites or (particularly in late spring) a grass seed in his ear canal.

If your Dachshund is not scratching and it is just a case of slightly dirty ears, you will be able to clean them yourself, using a suitable liquid or powder available at your local pet store. With the liquid solution, squeeze a few drops, as directed on the instructions, into the ear canal. Gently massage the ear to ensure the liquid is worked well into the problem area, and then gently wipe it out with either a soft cloth or a cotton bud. You might need somebody to hold and reassure him while you do this. You should be very careful not to probe too deeply in case you damage the ear canal; the use of cotton buds is best avoided for this reason.

With Long and Wire Dachshunds, you may find that there is hair growing in the ear and this could become a source of problems. Occasionally, you will need to pluck out this hair gently, using your thumb and forefinger.

EYES

The Dachshund should have a medium-sized, almond-shaped eye and, as such, is less prone to some of the eye problems found in other, more 'goggle-eyed', breeds. Eyes should be clear and bright with no sticky mess in the corners. Wipe any slight discharge and keep a look out for any recurrence, which may need to be referred to your vet. Also, look out for any redness in the eyelids, which may be a sign of infection or a foreign object, such as a grass seed, in which case a trip to the vet will be needed.

FOOT CARE

Accustom your Dachshund to nail-trimming from an early age.

In Wires and Long-coats you may need to trim the hair that grows between the pads.

NAILS

Depending on the shape of your Dachshund's feet and the type of surface on which he is exercised, you may need to trim his nails. If you are very lucky, he may keep his nails to a sensible length through exercise and you will not need to intervene. However, most Dachshunds will need their nails trimming at some time. Dew claws, located on the inside of the front legs (like thumbs) and occasionally on the inside of hind legs, may also need trimming.

Your puppy's breeder will almost certainly have started trimming his nails at a few weeks old, to prevent him from scratching and hurting his mother when feeding from her. If you continue trimming on a regular basis, he will get into the habit of allowing you to do it

without too much resistance. This can, however, be a two-person job: one person to hold the dog and one to wield your chosen implement, which could be a file, guillotine nail-cutters or a hand-held rotary grinding tool. If you do not get your dog accustomed to nail trimming on a regular basis, it is more likely that he will be very reluctant and you will have to ask your vet, or vet nurse, to do this for you.

You only need to trim the tips of the nails, but great care is needed to avoid cutting into the quick. If you do cut the quick, it usually leads to profuse bleeding, which you can stem with a firmly applied tissue and use of a styptic pencil.

While you are checking your Dachshund's nails, have a look between the pads of his feet and ensure there are no mud-balls, which can make it painful to walk. Carefully cut out any mud-balls or tangled hair with a pair of sharp, narrow-bladed scissors. Grass seeds can also get between the toes and cause inflammation; if one gets in too far, your vet may need to operate to remove it.

TEETH

Dachshunds have large, powerful teeth for such a relatively small dog. They needed these for their original purpose of holding prey when working. Get your Dachshund into the routine of having his teeth brushed once a week. You can use an old human toothbrush, but only use doggy toothpaste, which can be bought in various palatable flavours.

Regular brushing will help prevent the build-up of tartar on your Dachshund's teeth, which otherwise will cause decay and bad breath. Make sure you brush right to the back of each side of his mouth, not just his front teeth.

If your Dachshund does have particularly bad breath, it may be worth consulting your vet to see if there is some underlying condition, such as gum problems, or he may recommend a change of diet.

Synthetic (nylon) bones are a useful toy to help your Dachshund maintain clean, strong and healthy teeth. They are available in most pet stores. Fresh bones are also useful for this purpose, but are best given outdoors, as they can be rather messy. Never give your Dachshund cooked bones, as these can splinter and cause blockages.

COAT CARE

The different approaches to coat care for the three coat types were introduced in the previous chapter.

SMOOTH

Smooth Dachshunds have the easiest coats to look after: a quick polish with a hound-glove is basically all that is needed, but there are numerous potions you can buy to enhance the gleam, if you wish.

LONG

Longs will need regular combing and brushing to avoid and remove tangles. The coat should be soft and straight, or only slightly waved. It should not be

Teeth should be cleaned on a regular basis.

fluffy. Lots of specialist grooming products are available to help you keep a long coat in top condition.

WIRE

Wire Dachshunds have a double-coat. There is a longer, harsh topcoat with a dense undercoat beneath. Two or three times a year the long, dead topcoat will need to be plucked out (hand-stripping) to allow the new topcoat to grow in. Wires have the advantage of not moulting like other dogs. If you are lucky enough to have a Wire with a short, harsh 'pin wire' coat, it will probably not need stripping at all. Pin Wires typically have little or no face furnishings, but still have a double coat, only shorter and harsher in texture than a 'normal' Wire coat. You will just need to tidy it up with a stiff brush to help remove dead hair.

You can take your pet Wire to a grooming parlour to have his coat hand-stripped (never clippered) or you can, with time and patience, do it yourself. If you decide to do it yourself, choose a time when the dog is relaxed and lying quietly beside you.
• Start at the neck, raising a fold of skin with one hand – you will see the long hairs of the topcoat standing away from the woolly undercoat.
• Take a few of the long, topcoat hairs between the

GROOMING YOUR DACHSHUND

SMOOTH COATS

Work through the coat with a soft bristle brush.

A polish will bring out the shine in the coat.

LONG COATS

You will need to use a slicker brush for a Long-haired Dachshund.

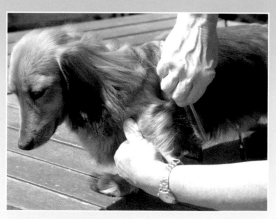

The coat should be combed through, easing out any knots or tangles in the feathering.

WIRE COATS

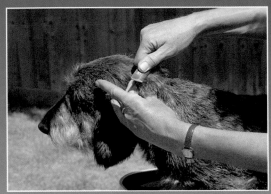

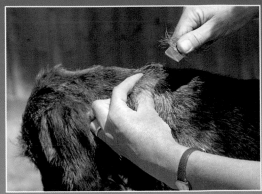

Using a stripping knife, start at the neck and gently pull out the dead hairs of the topcoat.

Continue working along the length of the back.

Move down to the hindquarters...

...and along to the tail.

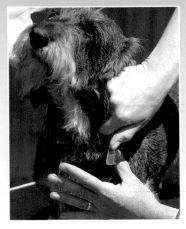

Move round to the front and work on the chest.

Each leg must be stripped.

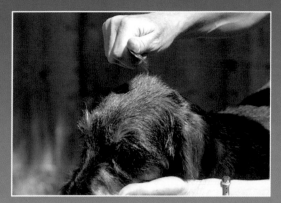

Now start work on the head.

The ears will need attention.

Finally, strip the beard.

The finished job.

finger and thumb of your
other hand, and pluck them
out. If the coat is ready to
come out, the topcoat will
come away easily without
distressing the dog.
- Continue down one side of
the dog, then the other and
down the back, until the dog
is in his undercoat all over.
This could take several
sessions, over a few days, to
achieve. Be kind, firm and
patient at all times.
- Finally, tidy the tail and legs
with a stripping knife (a blade
between two combs), which
can be obtained from pet
shops and dog shows.

BATHING

Dachshunds do have an
uncanny knack of finding
despicable (usually dead) things
to roll in when out walking in
the countryside. So, it is almost
inevitable that you will need to
bath yours when this happens.
Make sure you use a dedicated
dog shampoo; many of these
contain insecticidal agents,
which help prevent flea or mite
infestations. You can ask your
puppy's breeder what shampoo
best suits the coat type.

A Miniature can probably be
bathed in the kitchen or utility-
room sink. For a Standard, you
can either use your own bath, or
probably more practically, a
plastic baby-bath, which you can
fill from a bucket.

NEUTERING

Breeding puppies is a highly
specialised business, and if this is
your intention, you will need to
do a huge amount of homework
before getting involved.

The majority of pet owners do
not want to breed from their dogs
so, therefore, neutering is an
option that should be
considered. Many veterinary
surgeons advocate this, but it is
not a straightforward or obvious
decision to make. Neutering is a
major operation for bitches and
has its associated risks, so you
will have to weigh up the pros
and cons.

SPAYING

If you are thinking of getting your
bitch spayed, you should ask
your vet for advice on the best
age to do this. Generally, the
advice is not to have a bitch
spayed before her first season.
The number of health benefits
associated with spaying a bitch
may exceed the associated health
problems in many cases.

Bitches can benefit from
spaying by reducing the
incidence of uterine or ovarian
cancers; it also prevents them
from getting uterine infections
later in life. An infected uterus,
called pyometra, is a serious and
potentially fatal infection.

Spaying can soften the coat texture of a Wire and spayed bitches tend to be more prone to putting on extra weight.

CASTRATION

Neutering a male reduces the incidences of prostate and testicular cancer. Castrated male Dachshunds are less likely to develop unwanted behaviours, such as marking of territory, sexual aggression, and mounting. You should not have a dog castrated before he is mature (i.e. some time after he has started cocking his leg).

CARING FOR AN ELDERLEY DACHSHUND

A recent health survey showed the average age of death of Dachshunds was over 11 years. Standards can easily reach this age and Miniatures typically go on much longer; 14 and 15 is not unusual.

As your Dachshund grows older, beyond the age of seven, he will gradually slow down and be slightly less inclined to want the vigorous exercise he enjoyed as a youngster. As we described in the earlier discussion on nutrition, you will need to regulate his diet accordingly. As he burns less energy, you should feed him a lower-protein/lower-fat diet, and maybe also reduce the quantities you give him.

Watch your dog's weight and do not allow him to become obese, as this will put unnecessary pressure on his

bones and vital organs.

He still needs his exercise, but you should not expect him to walk as far; his mind may be willing, but his body will not be quite so able to cope and you can overdo it. Allow him to grow old gracefully, taking time to do the things he really enjoys, at his pace.

An elderly Dachshund may well lose his sight and/or hearing and you will have to make allowances for this in his, and in your, daily routine.

Unless he dies peacefully through old age, knowing when to say goodbye to your Dachshund is probably one of the most difficult decisions you will ever have to make. If he has been having regular checks, your vet will be able to give you an objective opinion on when the time is approaching. Only you can make the final decision, but it is important to remember that you have to do whatever is in the best interest of your Dachshund. If his quality of life has deteriorated, it is no kindness to prolong his life just to satisfy your needs.

You will grieve for your Dachshund when the time comes, but you will have so many fond memories to cherish.

The older dog deserves special care and consideration.

SOCIALISATION & TRAINING

Chapter 6

When you decided to bring a Dachshund into your life, you probably had dreams of how it was going to be: long walks together, cosy evenings with a Dachshund lying devotedly at your feet and, whenever you returned home, there would always be a special welcome waiting for you.

There is no doubt that you can achieve all this – and much more – with a Dachshund, but like anything that is worth having, you must be prepared to put in the work. A Dachshund, regardless of whether he is a puppy or an adult, does not come ready trained, understanding exactly what you want and fitting perfectly into your lifestyle. A Dachshund has to learn his place in your family and he must discover what is acceptable behaviour.

We have a great starting point in that the breed has an outgoing temperament. The Dachshund was developed to be a working dog and although he retains an independent outlook on life, he also enjoys interacting with his human family. He is also highly intelligent – which is not the same as saying he is easy to train – but this is a hound with a brain, so you must be on your mettle in order to bring out the best in him. Watch out for the Dachshund sense of humour, which is a hallmark of the breed and can catch you off your guard!

With six varieties to choose from, there are some differences in temperament – and advocates for each variety will claim that theirs is the most sweet-natured, loyal, quick-witted…

As a generalisation, Wires are the most extrovert and active, Standard Longs are the most laid-back, and Standard Smooths are perhaps more 'one person' or 'one family' dogs. All the Miniatures make ideal pets for someone who is less active and who wants a small but affectionate companion.

THE FAMILY PACK

Dogs have been domesticated for some 14,000 years but, luckily for us, they have inherited and retained behaviour from their distant ancestor – the wolf. A Dachshund may never have lived in the wild, but he is born with the survival skills and the mentality of a meat-eating predator who hunts in a pack. A wolf living in a pack owes its existence to mutual co-operation and an acceptance of a hierarchy, as this ensures both food and protection. A domesticated dog living in a family pack has exactly the same outlook. He wants food, companionship, and leadership – and it is your job to provide for these needs.

Do you have what it takes to be a firm, fair and consistent leader?

YOUR ROLE

Theories about dog behaviour and methods of training go in and out of fashion, but in reality, nothing has changed from the day when wolves ventured in from the wild to join the family circle. The wolf (and equally the dog) accepts a subservient place in the family pack in return for food and protection. In a dog's eyes, you are his leader and he relies on you to make all the important decisions. This does not mean that you have to act like a dictator or a bully. You are accepted as a leader, without argument, as long as you have the right credentials.

The first part of the job is easy. You are the provider and you are therefore respected because you supply food. In a Dachshund's eyes, you must be the ultimate hunter, because a day never goes by when you cannot find food. The second part of the leader's job description is straightforward, but for some reason we find it hard to achieve. In order for a dog to accept his place in the family pack, he must respect his leader as the decision-maker. A low-ranking pack animal does not question authority; he is perfectly happy to see someone else shoulder the responsibility. Problems will only arise if you cut a poor figure as leader and the dog feels he should mount a challenge for the top-ranking role.

Owners of small dogs are often lulled into a false state of complacency, thinking there is no need to train a dog of this size. After all, you can always pick him up if he doesn't want to co-operate! But with a Dachshund, you need to bear in mind that you are dealing with a hound – not a toy dog. A hound was bred to hunt, and a Dachshund – even a Miniature – has inherited a good nose coupled with keenness, independence and determination. If you do not keep these characteristics in check, you will have a dog that is intent on pleasing himself rather than co-operating with you.

HOW TO BE A GOOD LEADER

There are a number of guidelines to follow to establish yourself in the role of leader in a way that your Dachshund understands and respects. If you have a puppy, you may think you don't have to take this on board for a few months, but that would be a big mistake. With a Dachshund it is essential to start as you mean to go on. The behaviour he learns as a puppy will continue throughout his adult life, which means that undesirable behaviour can be very difficult to rectify.

When your Dachshund first arrives in his new home, follow these guidelines:

• **Keep it simple:** Decide on the rules you want your Dachshund to obey and always make it 100 per cent clear what is acceptable, and what is unacceptable, behaviour.

• **Be consistent:** If you are not consistent about enforcing rules, how can you expect your Dachshund to take you seriously? There is nothing worse than allowing your Dachshund to jump on the sofa one moment and then scolding him the next time he does it because he is muddy. As far as the Dachshund is concerned, he may as well try it on because he can't predict your reaction. Bear in mind, inconsistency leads to insecurity.

• **Get your timing right:** If you are rewarding your Dachshund and, equally, if you are reprimanding him, you must respond within one to two seconds otherwise the dog will not link his behaviour with your reaction (see page 88).

• Read your dog's body language: Find out how to read body language and facial expressions (see page 87) so that you understand your Dachshund's feelings and intentions.

• **Be aware of your own body language:** You can also help your dog to learn by using your body language to communicate with him. For example, if you want your dog to come to you, open your arms out and look inviting. If you want your dog to stay, use a hand signal (palm flat, facing the dog) so you are effectively 'blocking' his advance.

• **Tone of voice:** Dogs do not speak English; they learn by associating a word with the required action. However, they are very receptive to tone of voice, so you can use your voice to praise him or to correct undesirable behaviour. If you are pleased with your Dachshund, praise him to the skies in a warm, happy voice. If you want to stop him raiding the bin, use a deep, stern voice when you say "No".

• **Give one command only:** If you keep repeating a command, or keep changing it, your Dachshund will think you are babbling and will probably ignore

you. If your Dachshund does not respond the first time you ask, make it simple by using a treat to lure him into position and then you can reward him for a correct response.

• **Daily reminders:** A young, independent-minded Dachshund is apt to forget his manners from time to time and an adolescent dog may attempt to challenge your authority (see page 100). Rather than coming

Most dogs will respond more readily to body language than to verbal cues.

If you watch dogs interacting, you will learn to read their body language. This youngster is adopting an "I am no threat" policy.

One adult decides to assert his authority a little more forcibly.

Job done – the youngster is now free to go, having received the message loud and clear that the adult dog must be respected.

down on your Dachshund like a ton of bricks when he does something wrong, try to prevent bad manners by daily reminders of good manners. For example:

i.   Do not let your dog barge ahead of you when you are going through a door.

ii.   Do not let him leap out of the car the moment you open the door (which could be potentially lethal, as well as being disrespectful).

iii.   Do not let your Dachshund eat from your hand when you are at the table.

iv.   Do not let him 'win' a toy at the end of a play session and then make off with it. You 'own' his toys and you 'allow' him to play with them. Your Dachshund must learn to give up a toy when you ask.

UNDERSTANDING YOUR DACHSHUND

Body language is an important means of communication between dogs, which they use to make friends, to assert status and to avoid conflict. It is important to get on your dog's wavelength by understanding his body language and reading his facial expressions.

- A positive body posture and a wagging tail indicate a happy, confident dog.
- A crouched body posture with ears back and tail down show that a dog is being submissive. A dog may do this when he is being told off or if a more assertive dog approaches him.
- A bold dog will stand tall, looking strong and alert. His ears will be forward and his tail will be held high.
- A dog who raises his hackles (lifting the fur along his topline) is trying to look as scary as possible.
- A playful dog will go down on his front legs while standing on his hind legs in a bow position. This friendly invitation says: "I'm no threat, let's play."
- A dominant, aggressive dog will meet other dogs with a hard stare. If he is challenged, he may bare his teeth and growl, and the corners of his mouth will be drawn forward. His ears will be forward and he will appear tense in every muscle.
- A nervous dog will often show aggressive behaviour as a means of self-protection. If threatened, this dog will lower his head and flatten his ears.

The corners of his mouth may be drawn back and he may bark or whine.

GIVING REWARDS

Why should your Dachshund do as you ask? If you follow the guidelines given above, your Dachshund should respect your authority, but what about the time when he is on the trail of a really enticing scent? The answer is that you must always be the most interesting, the most attractive, and the most irresistible person in your Dachshund's eyes. It would be nice to think that you could achieve this by personality alone, but most of us need a little extra help. You need to find out what is the biggest reward for your dog. In most cases, a Dachshund will be motivated to work for food reward, although some enjoy a game with a toy. This is

more likely to be the case if a Dachshund has had lots of opportunity to play with toys as he is growing up, and sees a toy as a chance for an interactive game with his owner. But, whatever reward you use, make sure it is something that your dog really wants.

When you are teaching a dog a new exercise, you should reward your Dachshund frequently. When he knows the exercise or command, reward him randomly so that he keeps on responding to you in a positive manner. The Dachshund is very quick to learn, but he may 'switch off' when he thinks he has done enough. A system of random rewards will help to keep him guessing, and therefore keep him focused.

If your Dachshund does something extra special, like leaving a scent trail when he hears you calling him, make sure

For most Dachshunds, a food reward is viewed as a top treat.

There are some dogs who see a game with a toy as the best reward.

he really knows how pleased you are by giving him a handful of treats or throwing his ball a few extra times. If he gets a jackpot reward, he is more likely to come back on future occasions because you have proved to be even more rewarding than his previous activity.

TOP TREATS

Some trainers grade treats depending on what they are asking the dog to do. A dog may get a low-grade treat (such as a piece of dry food) to reward good behaviour on a random basis, such as sitting when you open a door or allowing you to examine his teeth. High-grade treats

(which may be cooked liver, sausage or cheese) may be reserved for training new exercises, or for use in the park when you want a really good recall, for example.

Whatever type of treat you use, you should remember to subtract it from your Dachshund's daily food ration. Dachshunds can be prone to obesity. Fat dogs are lethargic, prone to health problems and will almost certainly have a shorter life-expectancy, so reward your Dachshund, but always keep a check on his figure!

HOW DO DOGS LEARN?

It is not difficult to get inside

your Dachshund's head and understand how he learns, as it is not dissimilar to the way we learn. Dogs learn by conditioning: they find out that specific behaviours produce specific consequences. This is known as operant conditioning or consequence learning. Consequences have to be immediate or clearly linked to the behaviour, as a dog sees the world in terms of action and result. Dogs will quickly learn if an action has a bad consequence or a good consequence.

Dogs also learn by association. This is known as classical conditioning or association learning. It is the type of learning

THE CLICKER REVOLUTION

Karen Pryor pioneered the technique of clicker training when she was working with dolphins. It is very much a continuation of Pavlov's work and makes full use of association learning. Karen wanted to mark 'correct' behaviour at the precise moment it happened. She found it was impossible to toss a fish to a dolphin when it was in mid-air, when she wanted to reward it. Her aim was to establish a conditioned response so the dolphin knew that it had performed correctly and a reward would follow.

The solution was the clicker: a small matchbox-shaped training aid, with a metal tongue that makes a click when it is pressed. To begin with, the dolphin had to learn that a click meant that food was coming. The dolphin then learnt that it must 'earn' a click in order to get a reward. Clicker training has been used with many different animals, most particularly with dogs, and it has proved hugely successful. It is a great aid for pet owners and is also widely used by professional trainers who teach highly specialised skills.

made famous by Pavlov's experiment with dogs. Pavlov presented dogs with food and measured their salivary response (how much they drooled). Then he rang a bell just before presenting the food. At first, the dogs did not salivate until the food was presented. But after a while they learnt that the sound of the bell meant that food was coming and so they salivated when they heard the bell. A dog needs to learn the association in order for it to have any meaning. For example, a dog that has never seen a lead before will be completely indifferent to it. A dog that has learnt that a lead means he is going for a walk will get excited the second he sees the lead; he has learnt to associate a lead with a walk.

BE POSITIVE

The most effective method of training dogs is to use their ability to learn by consequence and to teach that the behaviour you want produces a good consequence. For example, if you ask your Dachshund to "Sit" and reward him with a treat, he will learn that it is worth his while to sit on command because it will lead to a treat. He is far more likely to repeat the behaviour and the behaviour will become stronger, because it results in a positive outcome. This method of training is known as positive reinforcement and it generally leads to a happy, co-operative dog that is willing to work and a handler who has fun training their dog.

The opposite approach is negative reinforcement. This is far less effective and often results in a poor relationship between dog and owner. In this method of training, you ask your Dachshund to "Sit" and if he does not respond, you deliver a sharp yank on the training collar or push his rear to the ground. The dog learns that not responding to your command has a bad consequence and he may be less likely to ignore you in the future. However, it may well have a bad consequence for you, too. A dog that is treated in this way may associate harsh handling with the handler and become aggressive or fearful. Instead of establishing a pattern of willing co-operation, you are establishing a relationship built on coercion.

GETTING STARTED

As you train your Dachshund you will develop your own techniques as you get to know what motivates him. You may decide to get involved with clicker training or you may prefer to go for a simple command-and-reward formula. It does not matter what form of training you use, as long as it is based on positive, reward-based methods.

There are a few important guidelines to bear in mind when you are training your Dachshund:

- Find a training area that is free from distractions, particularly when you are just starting out. A Dachshund loves to use his nose, so it may be easier to train him indoors or in your garden to begin with.
- Keep training sessions short, especially with young puppies that have very short attention spans.
- Do not train if you are in a bad mood or if you are on a tight schedule – the training session will be doomed to failure.
- If you are using a toy as a reward, make sure it is only available when you are training. In this way it has an added value for your Dachshund.
- If you are using food treats, make sure they are bite-size and easy to swallow; you don't want to hang about while your Dachshund chews on his treat.
- Do not attempt to train your Dachshund after he has eaten, or soon after returning from exercise. He will either be too full up to care about food treats or too tired to concentrate.
- When you are training, move around your allocated area so that your dog does not think that an exercise can only be performed in one place.
- If your Dachshund is finding an exercise difficult, try not to get frustrated. Go back a step and praise him for his effort. You will probably find he is more successful when you try

The Dachshund loves to use his nose, so you may find it easier to start training in the house where there are fewer distractions.

It will not take your Dachshund long to learn that a 'click' means that a reward will follow.

again at the next training session.

- If a training session is not going well – either because you are in the wrong frame of mind or the dog is not focusing – ask your Dachshund to do something you know he can do (such as a trick he enjoys performing) and then you can reward him with a food treat or a play with his favourite toy, ending the session on a happy, positive note.
- Do not train for too long. You need to end a training session on a high, with your Dachshund wanting more, rather than making him sour by asking too much from him.

In the exercises that follow, clicker training is introduced and followed, but all the exercises will work without the use of a clicker.

INTRODUCING A CLICKER

This is dead easy, and the intelligent Dachshund will learn about the clicker in record time! It can be combined with attention training, which is a very useful tool and can be used on many different occasions.

- Prepare some treats and go to an area that is free from distractions. Allow your Dachshund to wander, and, when he stops to look at you, click and reward by throwing him a treat. This means he will not crowd you, but will go looking for the treat. Repeat a couple of times. If your Dachshund is very easily distracted, you may need to start this exercise with the dog on a lead.
- After a few clicks, your Dachshund will understand that if he hears a click, he will get a treat. He must now learn that he must 'earn' a click. This time, when your Dachshund looks at you, wait a little longer before clicking and then reward him. If your Dachshund is on a lead but responding well, try him off the lead.
- When your Dachshund is working for a click and giving you his attention, you can introduce a cue or command word, such as "Watch". Repeat a few times, using the cue. You now have a Dachshund that understands the clicker and will give you his attention when you ask him to "Watch".

TRAINING EXERCISES

If you want a dog that's going to be easy to train, buy a gundog or a Border Collie, not a Dachshund. Dachshunds are not noted for their obedience but, with patience and persistence by the owner, they can be trained to basic levels of obedience. Most important of all, keep training sessions fun so your Dachshund enjoys the quality time he is spending with you.

THE SIT

This is the easiest exercise to teach, so it is rewarding for both you and your Dachshund. The conformation of the Dachshund, with his long body, means that sitting is not the most comfortable position for him to adopt, so do not expect him to stay in position for too long.
- Choose a tasty treat and hold it just above your puppy's nose. As he looks up at the treat, he will naturally go into the 'Sit'. As soon as he is in position, reward him.
- Repeat the exercise and when your pup understands what you want, introduce the "Sit" command.
- You can practise the Sit exercise at mealtimes by holding out the bowl and waiting for your dog to sit. Most Dachshunds learn this one very quickly!

THE DOWN

Work hard at this exercise because a reliable 'Down' is useful in many different situations, and an instant 'Down' can be a lifesaver.
- You can start with your dog in a 'Sit', or it is just as effective to teach it when the dog is standing. Hold a treat just below your puppy's nose and slowly lower it towards the ground. The treat acts as a lure and your puppy will follow it, first going down on his forequarters and then bringing his hindquarters down as he tries to get the treat.
- Make sure you close your fist around the treat and only reward your puppy with the treat when he is in the correct position. If your puppy is reluctant to go 'Down', you can apply gentle pressure on his shoulders to encourage him to go into the correct position.
- When your puppy is following the treat and going into position, introduce a verbal command.
- Build up this exercise over a period of time, each time waiting a little longer before giving the reward, so the puppy learns to stay in the 'Down' position.

With practice, your Dachshund will respond to a verbal cue to "Sit".

Lure your Dachshund into the Down position.

THE RECALL

It is never too soon to begin recall training. The Dachshund is a hound, and his greatest delight is to find a scent and follow it. All his instincts are telling him to do this, so it is not surprising that many Dachshund owners complain that their dog 'goes deaf' when he is on a scent trail.

The only way to overcome this problem is to make yourself more exciting so your Dachshund is motivated to leave what he is doing and come to you. It takes time and patience to establish a reliable recall, but it is well worth the effort for both you and your dog. You will be able to give your Dachshund free runs where he has the opportunity to use his nose to his heart's content, knowing he will come back to you when you call him.

Hopefully, the breeder will have already started recall training by calling the puppies in from outside and rewarding them with some treats scattered on the floor. But even if this has not been the case, you will find that a puppy arriving in his new home is highly responsive. His chief desire is to follow you and be with you.

Capitalise on this from day one by getting your pup's attention and calling him to you in a bright, excited tone of voice.

- Practise in the garden. When your puppy is busy exploring, get his attention by calling his name, and, as he runs towards you, introduce the verbal command "Come". Make sure you sound happy and exciting, so your puppy wants to come to you. When he responds, give him lots of praise.

- If your puppy is slow to respond, try running away a few paces or jumping up and

Make yourself sound really exciting so your Dachshund wants to come to you.

down. It doesn't matter how silly you look, the key issue is to get your puppy's attention and then make yourself irresistible!

• In a dog's mind, coming when called should be regarded as the best fun because he knows he is always going to be rewarded. Never make the mistake of telling your dog off, no matter how slow he is to respond, as you will undo all your previous hard work.

• When you call your Dachshund to you, make sure he comes up close enough to be touched. He must understand that "Come" means that he should come right up to you, otherwise he will think that he can approach and then veer off when it suits him.

• When you are free-running your dog, make sure you have his favourite toy or a pocket full of treats so you can reward him at intervals throughout the walk when you call him to you. If you are using food as a reward, make sure you have some high-value treats, such as liver or sausage, so your Dachshund learns that coming back to you is really worth his while.

• If your Dachshund responds to your call instantly (for a Dachshund!) or comes from a long way off, give him a jackpot reward when he comes

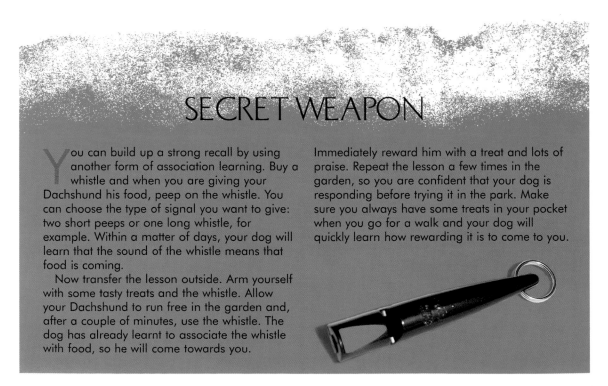

SECRET WEAPON

You can build up a strong recall by using another form of association learning. Buy a whistle and when you are giving your Dachshund his food, peep on the whistle. You can choose the type of signal you want to give: two short peeps or one long whistle, for example. Within a matter of days, your dog will learn that the sound of the whistle means that food is coming.

Now transfer the lesson outside. Arm yourself with some tasty treats and the whistle. Allow your Dachshund to run free in the garden and, after a couple of minutes, use the whistle. The dog has already learnt to associate the whistle with food, so he will come towards you.

Immediately reward him with a treat and lots of praise. Repeat the lesson a few times in the garden, so you are confident that your dog is responding before trying it in the park. Make sure you always have some treats in your pocket when you go for a walk and your dog will quickly learn how rewarding it is to come to you.

to you, sprinkling high-value treats on the ground. Remember to back this up with lots of verbal praise so your Dachshund understands he has been a really good boy!

- Do not allow your dog to run free and only call him back at the end of the walk to clip on his lead. An intelligent Dachshund will soon realise that the recall means the end of his walk and then end of fun – so who can blame him for not wanting to come back?

TRAINING LINE
This is the equivalent of a very long lead, which you can buy at a pet store, or you can make your own with a length of rope. The training line is attached to your Dachshund's collar and should be around 15 feet (4.5 metres) in length.

The purpose of the training line is to prevent your Dachshund from disobeying you so that he never has the chance to get into bad habits. For example, when you call your Dachshund and he ignores you, you can immediately pick up the end of the training line and call him again. By picking up the line you will have attracted his attention and if you

The aim is for your Dachshund to walk on a loose lead, giving attention when required.

call in an excited, happy voice, your Dachshund will come to you. The moment he reaches you, give him a tasty treat so he is instantly rewarded for making the 'right' decision.

The training line is very useful when your Dachshund becomes an adolescent and is testing your leadership. When you have reinforced the correct behaviour a number of times, your dog will build up a strong recall and you will not need to use a training line.

WALKING ON A LOOSE LEAD
This is a simple exercise, and if you spend time working on it in the early stages, you will be rewarded with a dog that is happy to walk alongside you, neither pulling ahead nor lagging behind. As with so many aspects of dog training, it is so much better to establish good habits rather than trying to retrain a dog who has got into bad habits.

In this exercise, as with all lessons that you teach your Dachshund, you must adopt a calm, determined, no-nonsense attitude so he knows that you mean business. Once this is established, your Dachshund will take you seriously and be happy to co-operate with you.

- In the early stages of lead training, allow your puppy to pick his route and follow him. He will get used to the feeling of being 'attached' to you and will have no reason to put up any resistance.
- Next, find a toy or a tasty treat and show it to your puppy. Let him follow the treat/toy for a few paces and then reward him.
- Build up the amount of time your pup will walk with you, and, when he is walking nicely

by your side, introduce the verbal command "Heel" or "Close". Give lots of praise when your pup is in the correct position.

- When your pup is walking alongside you, keep focusing his attention on you by using his name and then rewarding him when he looks at you. If it is going well, introduce some changes of direction.

- Do not attempt to take your puppy out on the lead until you have mastered the basics at home. You need to be confident that your puppy accepts the lead and will focus his attention on you, when requested, before you face the challenge of a busy environment.

- If you are heading somewhere special, such as the park, your Dachshund may try to pull because he is impatient to get there. If this happens, stop, call your dog to you and do

not set off again until he is in the correct position. It may take time, but your Dachshund will eventually realise that it is more productive to walk by your side than to pull ahead.

STAYS

This may not be the most exciting exercise, but it is one of the most useful. There are many occasions when you want your Dachshund to stay in position, even if it is only for a few seconds. The classic example is when you want your Dachshund to stay in the back of the car until you have clipped on his lead.

Some trainers use the verbal command "Stay" when the dog is to stay in position for an extended period of time and "Wait" if the dog is to stay in position for a few seconds until you give the next command. Others trainers use a universal "Stay" to cover all situations. It

all comes down to personal preference, and as long as you are consistent, your dog will understand the command he is given.

The Dachshund is such a lively, alert little dog that he can be easily distracted when he is asked to "Stay." The key is to build up this exercise gradually, and do not ask your Dachshund to stay in position too long. The aim is to reward him for a good "Stay" rather than allowing him to break position.

- Put your puppy in a 'Sit' or a 'Down' and use a hand signal (flat palm, facing the dog) to show he is to stay in position. Step a pace away from the dog. Wait a second, step back and reward him. If you have a lively pup, you may find it easier to train this exercise on the lead.

- Repeat the exercise, gradually increasing the distance you can leave your dog. When you return to your dog's side, praise him quietly and release him with a command, such as "OK".

- Remember to keep your body language very still when you are training this exercise and avoid eye contact with your dog. Work on this exercise over a period of time and you will build up a really reliable 'Stay'.

SOCIALISATION

While your Dachshund is mastering basic obedience exercises, there is other, equally important, work to do with him. A Dachshund is not only becoming a part of your home

Build up the Stay exercise in easy stages.

and family, he is becoming a member of the community. He needs to be able to live in the outside world, coping calmly with every new situation that comes his way. It is your job to introduce him to as many different experiences as possible and to encourage him to behave in an appropriate manner.

In order to socialise your Dachshund effectively, it is helpful to understand how his brain is developing and then you will get a perspective on how he sees the world.

CANINE SOCIALISATION
(Birth to 7 weeks)

This is the time when a dog learns how to be a dog. By interacting with his mother and his littermates, a young pup learns about leadership and submission. He learns to read body posture so that he understands the intentions of his mother and his siblings. A puppy that is taken away from his litter too early may always have behavioural problems with other dogs, either being fearful or aggressive.

SOCIALISATION PERIOD
(7 to 12 weeks)

This is the time to get cracking and introduce your Dachshund puppy to as many different experiences as possible. This includes meeting different people, other dogs and animals, seeing new sights and hearing a range of sounds, from the vacuum cleaner to the roar of traffic. It may be that your Dachshund has been reared in kennels; if this is the case, you must work even harder at this stage of his education. A puppy

The puppies learn their first lessons from their mother.

learns very quickly and what he learns will stay with him for the rest of his life. This is the best time for a puppy to move to a new home, as he is adaptable and ready to form deep bonds.

FEAR-IMPRINT PERIOD (8 to 11 weeks)

This occurs during the socialisation period and it can be the cause of problems if it is not handled carefully. If a pup is exposed to a frightening or painful experience, it will lead to lasting impressions. Obviously, you will attempt to avoid frightening situations, such as your pup being bullied by a mean-spirited older dog, or a firework going off, but you cannot always protect your puppy from the unexpected. If your pup has a nasty experience, the best plan is to make light of it and distract him by offering him a treat or a game. The pup will take the lead from you and will be reassured that there is nothing to worry about. If you mollycoddle him and sympathise with him, he is far more likely to retain the memory of his fear.

SENIORITY PERIOD (12 to 16 weeks)

During this period, your Dachshund puppy starts to cut the apron strings and becomes more independent. He will test out his status to find out who is the pack leader: him or you. Bad habits, such as play biting, which may have been seen as endearing a few weeks earlier, should be firmly discouraged. Remember to use positive, reward-based training, but make sure your puppy knows that you are the leader and must be respected.

SECOND FEAR-IMPRINT PERIOD (6 to 14 months)

This period is not as critical as the first fear-imprint period, but it should still be handled carefully. During this time your Dachshund may appear apprehensive, or he may show fear of something familiar. You may feel as if you have taken a backwards step, but if you adopt a calm, positive manner, your Dachshund will see that there is nothing to be frightened of. Do not make your dog confront the thing that frightens him. Simply distract his attention and give him something else to think about, such as obeying a simple command, such as "Sit" or "Down". This will give you the opportunity to praise and reward your dog and will help to boost his confidence.

YOUNG ADULTHOOD AND MATURITY (1 to 4 years)

The timing of this phase depends on the size of the dog: the bigger the dog, the later it is. This period coincides with a dog's increased size and strength, mental as well as physical. Some dogs, particularly those with a dominant nature, will test your leadership again and may become aggressive towards other dogs. Firmness and continued training are essential at this time, so that your Dachshund accepts his status in the family pack.

IDEAS FOR SOCIALISATION

When you are socialising your Dachshund, you want him to experience as many different situations as possible. Try out

A well-socialised dog is relaxed and happy in a variety of situations – at home and further afield.

some of the following ideas, which will ensure your Dachshund has an all-round education.

If you are taking on a rescued dog and have little knowledge of his background, it is important to work through a programme of socialisation. A young puppy soaks up new experiences like a sponge, but an older dog can still learn. If a rescued dog shows fear or apprehension, treat him in exactly the same way as you would treat a youngster who is going through the second fear-imprint period.

- Accustom your puppy to household noises, such as the vacuum cleaner, the television and the washing machine.
- Ask visitors to come to the door, wearing different types of clothing – for example, wearing a hat, a long raincoat, or carrying a stick or an umbrella.
- If you do not have children at home, make sure your Dachshund has a chance to meet and play with them. Go to a local park and watch children in the play area. You will not be able to take your Dachshund inside the play area, but he will see children playing and will get used to their shouts of excitement.
- Attend puppy classes. These are designed for puppies between the ages of 12 to 20 weeks and give puppies a chance to play and interact together in a controlled, supervised environment. Your vet will have details of a local class.
* Arrange to meet friends who have dogs that are of sound temperament. Give your Dachshund the opportunity to meet and greet the dogs and play with them. The Dachshund tends to see himself as a 'big dog', despite his size, and he may adopt a policy of 'bark first, and ask questions later'. If he is accustomed to meeting dogs who give off friendly, positive vibes, he will not need to put up such a front.
- Take a walk around some quiet streets, such as a residential area, so your Dachshund can get used to the sound of traffic. As he becomes more

TRAINING CLUBS

There are lots of training clubs to choose from. Your vet will probably have details of clubs in your area, or you can ask friends who have dogs if they attend a club. Alternatively, use the internet to find out more information. But how do you know if the club is any good?

Before you take your dog, ask if you can go to a class as an observer and find out the following:
- What experience does the instructor(s) have?
- Do they have experience with Dachshunds?
- Is the class well organised and are the dogs reasonably quiet? (A noisy class indicates an unruly atmosphere, which will not be conducive to learning.)
- Are there a number of classes to suit dogs of different ages and abilities?
- Are positive, reward-based training methods used?
- Does the club train for the Good Citizen Scheme (see page 106)?

If you are not happy with the training club, find another one. An inexperienced instructor who cannot handle a number of dogs in a confined environment can do more harm than good.

confident, progress to busier areas. Remember, your lead is like a live wire and your feelings will travel directly to your Dachshund. Assume a calm, confident manner and your puppy will take the lead from you and have no reason to be fearful.

• Go to a railway station. You don't have to get on a train if you don't need to, but your Dachshund will have the chance to experience trains, people wheeling luggage, loudspeaker announcements, and going up and down stairs and over railway bridges.

• If you live in the town, plan a trip to the country. You can enjoy a day out and provide an opportunity for your Dachshund to see livestock, such as sheep, cattle and horses.

• One of the best places for socialising a dog is at a country fair. There will be crowds of people, livestock in pens, tractors, bouncy castles, fairground rides and food stalls.

• When your dog is over 20 weeks of age, locate a training class for adult dogs. You may find that your local training class has both puppy and adult classes.

THE ADOLESCENT DACHSHUND

It happens to every dog – and every owner. One minute you have an obedient well-behaved youngster and the next you have an adolescent who appears to have forgotten everything he ever learnt.

A Dachshund male will start to show adolescent behaviour at any time between six months and nine months. In terms of behavioural changes, a male often becomes more assertive as he pushes the boundaries to see if he can achieve top-dog status. This applies to his attitude towards people and towards other dogs. If you are keeping two males together, problems may well arise at this time, particularly if one has been used at stud and the other hasn't. In most cases, a male will be fully mature at around 18 months to two years.

Female Dachshunds generally have their first season at any time

A Dachshund may experience some behavioural changes in adolescence.

between six and nine months. At this time, a female may become a little withdrawn, preferring her own company rather than interacting with those around her. Dachshund owners report that females seem to sleep more than usual just before, and during, their season. Some female Dachshunds are prone to false pregnancies, so you need to keep a close check for signs of unusual behaviour.

This can be a trying time, but it is important to retain a sense of perspective. Look at the situation from the dog's perspective and respond to uncharacteristic behaviour with firmness and consistency. Just like a teenager, an adolescent Dachshund feels the need to flex his muscles and challenge the status quo. This is a breed that is full of self-importance, and although you do not want to flatten your Dachshund, you need to make sure that you are the one who is in charge.

WHEN THINGS GO WRONG

Positive, reward-based training has proved to be the most effective method of teaching dogs, but what happens when your Dachshund does something wrong and you need to show him that his behaviour is unacceptable? The old-fashioned school of dog training used to rely on the powers of punishment and negative reinforcement. A dog who raided the bin, for example, was smacked. Now we have learnt that it is not only unpleasant and cruel to hit a dog,

it is also ineffective. If you hit a dog for stealing, he is more than likely to see you as the bad consequence of stealing, so he may raid the bin again, but probably not when you are around. If he raided the bin some time before you discovered it, he will be even more confused by your punishment, as he will not relate your response to his 'crime'.

A more commonplace example is when a dog fails to respond to a recall in the park. When the dog eventually comes back, the owner puts the dog on the lead and goes straight home to punish the dog for his poor response. Unfortunately, the dog will have a different interpretation. He does not think: "I won't ignore a recall command because the bad consequence is the end of my play in the park." He thinks: "Coming to my owner resulted in the end of playtime – therefore coming to my owner has a bad consequence, so I won't do that again."

There are a number of strategies to tackle undesirable behaviour – and they have nothing to do with harsh handling.

Ignoring bad behaviour: The Dachshund is a highly intelligent dog who likes to think for himself, so this can make him quite manipulative. For example, a young Dachshund that barks when you are preparing his food is showing his impatience and is attempting to train you, rather than the other way round. He

There are times when you need to halt your Dachshund in his tracks....

believes he can change a situation simply by making a noise – and even if he does not get his food any quicker, he is enjoying the attention he is getting when you shout at him to tell him to be quiet. He is getting the attention he wants, so why inhibit his behaviour?

In this situation, the best and most effective response is to ignore your Dachshund. Suspend food preparations and get on with another task, such as washing up. Do not go near the food or the food bowl again until your Dachshund is calm and quiet. Repeat this on every occasion when your Dachshund barks and he will soon learn that barking is non-productive. He is

If problems arise in behaviour, you will need to re-educate your Dachshund.

not rewarded with your attention – or with getting food. It will not take long for him to realise that being quiet is the most effective strategy. In this scenario, you have not only taught your Dachshund to be quiet when you are preparing his food, you have also earned his respect because you have taken control of the situation.

Stopping bad behaviour: There are occasions when you want to call an instant halt to whatever it is your Dachshund is doing. He may have just jumped on the sofa, or you may have caught him red-handed in the rubbish bin. He has already committed the 'crime', so your aim is to stop him and to redirect his attention. You can do this by using a deep, firm tone of voice to say "No", which will startle him, and then call him to you in a bright, happy

voice. If necessary, you can attract him with a toy or a treat. The moment your Dachshund stops the undesirable behaviour and comes towards you, you can reward his good behaviour. You can back this up by running through a couple of simple exercises, such as a 'Sit' or a 'Down' and rewarding with treats. In this way, your Dachshund focuses his attention on you and sees you as the greatest source of reward and pleasure.

In a more extreme situation, when you want to interrupt undesirable behaviour and you know that a simple "No" will not do the trick, you can try something a little more dramatic. If you get a can and fill it with pebbles, it will make a really loud noise when you shake it or throw it. The same effect can be achieved with purpose-made

training discs. The dog will be startled and stop what he is doing. Even better, the dog will not associate the unpleasant noise with you. This gives you the perfect opportunity to be the nice guy, calling the dog to you and giving him lots of praise.

PROBLEM BEHAVIOUR

If you have trained your Dachshund from puppyhood, survived his adolescence and established yourself as a fair and consistent leader, you will end up with a brilliant companion dog. A Dachshund is a well-balanced dog, who rarely has hang-ups if he has been correctly reared and socialised. Most Dachshunds are out-going, fun-loving and thrive on spending time with their owners. The most common cause of problem behaviour among Dachshunds is boredom and a lack of exercise. This breed is mentally active and requires mental stimulation. If this is lacking, a Dachshund will be quick to find his own agenda and will make his life more 'interesting' by becoming increasingly attention-seeking.

It may be that you have taken on a rescued Dachshund that has established behavioural problems. If you are worried about your Dachshund and feel out of your depth, do not delay in seeking professional help. This is readily available, usually through a referral from your vet, or you can find out additional information on the internet (see Appendices for web addresses). An animal behaviourist will have experience in tackling problem behaviour and will be able to help both you and your dog.

ASSERTIVE BEHAVIOUR

If you have trained and socialised your Dachshund correctly, he will know his place in the family pack and will have no desire to challenge your authority. As we have seen, adolescents may test the boundaries, but this behaviour will not continue if you exhibit the necessary leadership skills.

If you have taken on a rescued dog who has not been trained and socialised, or if you have let your adolescent Dachshund become over-assertive, you may find you have problems with a dog that is trying to get the upper hand.

Assertive behaviour is expressed in many different ways, which may include the following:

- Showing lack of respect for your personal space. For example, your dog will try to run through doors ahead of you or jump up at you.
- Ignoring basic obedience commands.
- Showing no respect to younger members of the family, pushing amongst them and completely ignoring them.
- Male dogs may start marking (cocking their leg) in the house.
- Aggression towards people or other dogs (see page 106).

However, the most common behaviour displayed by a Dachshund who has ideas above

his station is resource guarding. This may take a number of different forms:

- Getting up on to the sofa or your favourite armchair and growling when you tell him to get back on the floor.
- Becoming possessive over a toy, or guarding his food bowl by growling when you get too close.
- Growling when anyone approaches his bed or when anyone gets too close to where he is lying.

In each of these scenarios, the Dachshund has something he values and he aims to keep it. He does not have sufficient respect for you, his human leader, to give up what he wants and he is 'warning' you to keep away.

If a Dachshund lives with one person and has not been properly socialised, he may become possessive about 'his person' and this may make him over-protective.

If you see signs of your Dachshund trying to take control, you must work at lowering his status so that he realises that you are the leader and he must accept your authority. Although you need to be firm, you also need to use positive training methods so that your Dachshund is rewarded for the behaviour you want. In this way, his 'correct' behaviour will be strengthened and repeated.

The golden rule is not to become confrontational. The

A Dachshund may become possessive over his food bowl.

The best plan is to drop in some treats so your intervention is seen in a positive light.

dog will see this as a challenge and may become even more determined not to co-operate. Persistence is a Dachshund trait, and you do not want this expressed in a negative light.

There are a number of steps you can take to lower your Dachshund's status, which are far more likely to have a successful outcome. They include:

• Go back to basics and hold daily training sessions. Make sure you have some really tasty treats, or find a toy your Dachshund really values and only bring it out at training sessions. Run through all the training exercises you have taught your Dachshund. Remember, boredom is very often the key to undesirable behaviour. By giving him things to do, you are providing mental stimulation and you have the opportunity to make a big fuss of him and reward him when he does well. This will help to reinforce the message that you are the leader and that it is rewarding to do as you ask.

• Teach your Dachshund something new; this can be as simple as learning a trick, such as shaking paws. Having something new to think about will mentally stimulate your Dachshund and he will benefit from interacting with you.

• Be 100 per cent consistent with all house rules – your Dachshund must never jump on the sofa and you must never allow him to jump up at you.

• If your Dachshund is becoming possessive over toys, remove all his toys and keep them out of reach. It is then up to you to decide when to produce a toy and to initiate a game. Equally, it is you who will decide when the game is over and when to remove the toy. This teaches your Dachshund that you 'own' his toys. He has fun playing and interacting with you, but the game is over – and the toy is given up – when you say so.

• If your Dachshund has been guarding his food bowl, put the bowl down empty and drop in a little food at a time. Periodically stop dropping in the food and tell your Dachshund to "Sit" and "Wait". Give it a few seconds and then reward him by dropping in more food. This shows your Dachshund that

you are the provider of the food and he can only eat when you allow him to.

• Make sure the family eats before you feed your Dachshund. Some trainers advocate eating in front of the dog (maybe just a few bites from a biscuit) before starting a training session, so the dog appreciates your elevated status.

SEPARATION ANXIETY

A Dachshund should be brought up to accept short periods of separation from his owner so that he does not become anxious. A new puppy should be left for short periods on his own, ideally in a crate where he cannot get up to any mischief. It is a good idea to leave him with a boredom-busting toy so he will be happily occupied in your absence. When you return, do not rush to the

If a dog is not accustomed to spending time on his own, he may become anxious.

crate and make a huge fuss. Wait a few minutes, and then calmly go to the crate and release your dog, telling him how good he has been. If this scenario is repeated a number of times, your Dachshund will soon learn that being left on his own is no big deal.

If your Dachshund has been brought up to accept time on his own, it is rare for separation anxiety to develop. However, it may arise if you take on a rescued dog who has major insecurities. Separation anxiety is expressed in a number of ways and all are equally distressing for both dog and owner. An anxious dog who is left alone may bark and whine continuously, urinate and defecate, and may be extremely destructive.

There are a number of steps you can take when attempting to solve this problem.

- Put up a baby-gate between adjoining rooms and leave your dog in one room while you are in the other room. Your dog will be able to see you and hear you, but he is learning to cope without being right next to you. Build up the amount of time you can leave your dog in easy stages.
- Buy some boredom-busting toys and fill them with some tasty treats. Whenever you leave your dog, give him a food-filled toy so that he is busy while you are away.
- If you have not used a crate before, it is not too late to start. Make sure the crate is cosy and train your Dachshund

A kong stuffed with food will give your Dachshund an occupation while you are away.

to get used to going in his crate while you are in the same room. Gradually build up the amount of time he spends in the crate and then start leaving the room for short periods. When you return, do not make a fuss of your dog. Leave him for five or ten minutes before releasing him, so that he gets used to your comings and goings.

- Pretend to go out, putting on your coat and jangling your keys, but do not leave the house. An anxious dog often becomes hyped up by the ritual of leaving and this will

help to desensitize him.
- When you go out, leave a radio or a TV on. Some dogs are comforted by hearing voices and background noise when they are left alone.
- Try to make your absences as short as possible when you are first training your dog to accept being on his own.

If you take these steps, your dog should become less anxious and, over a period of time, you should be able to solve the problem. However, if you are failing to make progress, do not delay in calling in expert help.

NEW CHALLENGES

If you enjoy training your Dachshund, you may want to try one of the many dog sports that are now on offer. In the UK, we tend to allow certain breeds, such as Border Collies, German Shepherds and some of the gundog breeds, to dominate the world of competitive sports, but in the USA, owners of all breeds are keen to have a go. Your Dachshund may not make it all the way to the top – but you can both have a lot of fun working and training together.

GOOD CITIZEN SCHEME

This is a scheme run by the Kennel Club in the UK and the American Kennel Club in the USA. The schemes promote responsible ownership and help you to train a well-behaved dog who will fit in with the community. The schemes are excellent for all pet owners and they are also a good starting point if you plan to compete with your Dachshund when he is older. The KC and the AKC schemes vary in format. In the UK there are three levels: bronze, silver and gold, with each test becoming progressively more demanding. In the AKC scheme there is a single test.

The Good Citizen Scheme is taught at most training clubs. For more information, log on to the Kennel Club or AKC website (see Appendices).

SHOWING

In your eyes, your Dachshund is the most beautiful dog in the world – but would a judge agree? Showing is a highly competitive sport, demanding both time and money. However, many owners get bitten by the showing bug and their calendar is governed by the dates of the top showing fixtures.

To be successful in the show ring, a Dachshund must conform as closely as possible to the Breed Standard, which is a written blueprint describing the 'perfect' Dachshund (see Chapter Seven). To get started you need to buy a puppy that has show potential and then train him to perform in the ring. A Dachshund will be expected to stand in show pose,

AGGRESSION

Aggression is a complex issue, as there are different causes and the behaviour may be triggered by numerous factors. It may be directed towards people, but far more commonly it is directed towards other dogs. Aggression in dogs may be the result of:
• Assertive behaviour (see page 103).
• Defensive behaviour: This may be induced by fear, pain or punishment.
• Territory: A dog may become aggressive if strange dogs or people enter his territory (which is generally seen as the house and garden).
• Intra-sexual issues: This is aggression between sexes – male-to-male or female-to-female.
• Parental instinct: A mother dog may become aggressive if she is protecting her puppies.

The Dachshund should not have an aggressive bone in his body. This type of behaviour is only likely to appear if a dog has been allowed to rule his owner or he has not had the correct upbringing. This may happen if you have failed in your role as leader or, more commonly, if you have taken on an older, rescued dog that has been poorly socialised and may have undergone some traumatic experience.

If overly assertive behaviour is the underlying cause, you can try the measures outlined in this chapter. But if you are concerned about your dog's behaviour, you would be well advised to call in professional help. If the aggression is directed towards people, you should seek immediate advice. This behaviour can escalate very quickly and could lead to disastrous consequences.

If you want to get involved in showing you will need a Dachshund that conforms as closely as possible to the Breed Standard.

If you keep your Dachshund fit, he could become an agility competitor.

gait for the judge in order to show off his natural movement, and to be examined by the judge. This involves a detailed hands-on examination, so your Dachshund must be bombproof when handled by strangers. Many training clubs hold ringcraft classes, run by experienced showgoers, where you will learn how to handle your Dachshund in the ring, and you will also find out about rules, procedures and show-ring etiquette.

The best plan is to start off at some small, informal shows where you can practise and learn the tricks of the trade before graduating to bigger shows. It's a long haul starting in the very first puppy class, but the dream is to make your Dachshund into a Champion if he is good enough.

COMPETITIVE OBEDIENCE
It is rare to see a Dachshund compete in this sport in the UK, but you could always be a pioneer for the breed! The Dachshund is quick to learn; it is more a matter of keeping him focused and motivated.

In competitive obedience, there are various levels of achievement, starting with Beginners, but this is highly competitive, even at the lower levels. Marks are lost for even the slightest crooked angle noticed when the dog is sitting, and if a dog has a momentary attention deficit or works too far away from his owner in heelwork, again points will be deducted.

Even though competitive obedience requires accuracy and precision, make sure you make it fun for your Dachshund, with lots of praise and rewards so that you motivate him to do his best. Many training clubs run advanced classes for those who want to compete in obedience, or you can

hire the services of a professional trainer for one-on-one sessions.

AGILITY
This fun sport has grown enormously in popularity over the past few years. Again, the Dachshund may not be a natural choice but those that compete – mostly on breed club fun days – certainly seem to enjoy it. If you fancy having a go, make sure you have good control over your Dachshund and keep him slim. Agility is a very physical sport, which demands fitness from both dog and handler.

In agility competitions, each dog must complete a set course over a series of obstacles, which include:
• Jumps (upright hurdles and long jump, varying in height – small, medium and large, depending on the size of the dog)
• Weaves

- A-frame
- Dog walk
- See-saw
- Tunnels (collapsible and rigid)
- Tyre

Dogs may compete in Jumping classes, with jumps, tunnels and weaves, or in Agility classes, which have the full set of equipment. Faults are awarded for poles down on the jumps, missed contact points on the A-frame, dog walk and see-saw, and refusals. If a dog takes the wrong course, he is eliminated. The winner is the dog that completes the course in the fastest time with no faults. As you progress up the levels, courses become progressively harder with more twists, turns and changes of direction.

If you want to get involved in Agility, you will need to find a club that specialises in the sport (see Appendices). You will not be allowed to start training until your Dachshund is 12 months old, and you cannot compete until he is 18 months old. This rule is for the protection of the dog, who may suffer injury if he puts strain on bones and joints while he is still growing.

EARTHDOG TRIALS
Earthdog tests are one of the fastest-growing American Kennel Club (AKC) events for Dachshund

TRAINING YOUR WORKING TECKEL TO TRACK
Brenda Humphrey, Secretary, UK Teckel Stud Book Society

On many country estates where there are herds of deer, the Dachshund is highly regarded as a working dog who can make the tasks of managing the herd, such as tracking fallen deer, much easier. For anyone whose Dachshund is destined for a working life, training to follow a trail is essential. The UK Teckel Stud Book Society has many experienced owners who will be willing to help you learn how to teach your Dachshund to work properly. It is more common to use a Standard – rather than a Miniature – Dachshund for working with legal game. Your Dachshund can be taught to track any scent, animal or human.

Training can begin when your Dachshund is as young as four months old, and can be both fascinating and fun. When starting it should not be done any more than once or twice a week, as the pup will become bored. Training for following a trail should be combined with normal obedience training and socialisation for your Dachshund.

The use of a dog harness, with a pair of hawking bells attached, should always be used for training. In time this will excite the dog, as he will associate it with working. It is also useful to be able to hear where your dog is if he has disappeared into the undergrowth.

When first training, attach a lead to the harness and show your dog the trail. Start the training exercises with a command: "Where's the deer?" If he strays off the trail, pull him back on line, exciting him again with, "Find the deer!" Once the dog has got it right, start making the trail harder by increasing the distance, changing directions and eventually moving into woodland. As you progress to more complicated trails, mark them with triangles of paper on trees with a hand-held stapler.

Always trust your dog – a good dog knows best. Have fun!

owners and are yet another way to recognise the diverse skills that the breed displays. The AKC has made it possible for Dachshund owners to explore the talents of their dogs by drawing up a series of rules for conducting Earthdog tests. Interestingly, the Dachshund is the only hound breed eligible to compete in Earthdog trials; all the others are terrier breeds.

Any Dachshund over six months of age and who is registered at the AKC can compete at a range of levels, such as Junior, Senior and Master Earthdog. All the trials are conducted with man-made dens: wooden-sided tunnels with natural, smooth earth on the floor, buried just below ground level. Dens are constructed to ensure a safe environment for dogs, quarry, handlers and judges.

Depending on the level of the test, the dog must approach the den and enter it within a specified time before beginning to work the quarry. Working is defined as digging, barking, growling, lunging, and biting at the quarry cage. In the Senior level test, the dog must also respond to a recall from his handler after working the quarry, and in the Master level test, two dogs are worked together by their handler.

For more information, refer to the Dachshund Club of America website (see Appendices).

In the early stages of training, a long line is attached to the harness.

TRAINING YOUR WORKING TECKEL FOR HUNTING VERMIN
Sue Holt and Bernd Kugow (Waldmeister Miniature Wires)

Training begins by taking every opportunity to encourage the young dog to look for scent and track interesting smells. We often lay a trail of raw tripe juice along the grass for young puppies to follow. If they can keep on track, they are rewarded with a lump of tripe hidden somewhere in the garden. We also introduce them to tunnels and pipes as soon as they can walk, so that they become used to going through and coming back again. We use every opportunity to encourage them to be independent and to introduce them to interesting smells, sights and sounds.

From eight weeks old, the pups come up on to the moor with the older ones and we watch how they behave. Are they noticing smells and sounds? Will they go into cover and explore independently or are they frightened? It does not always click right away; you often have to give them time to assimilate the information they are gathering. But, with time and patience, their instinct usually comes to the surface. It is at this stage that they are trained to come back to the whistle. This is vitally important and can be crucial in avoiding danger. Our young pups usually respond by copying the older ones, who come back when the whistle is blown three times. If a pup does not respond to the whistle, we put him on a long field line and blow the whistle. If he ignores it, a good tug that stops him and brings him back towards the

handler will ensure he gets the message (eventually!). This method is also used on older dogs who may have become headstrong or have stopped coming back to the whistle.

The field line is also a necessary piece of equipment for training your Dachshund not to bother sheep. All our Dachshunds walk through fields of sheep on a daily basis and do not even look at them. This has been achieved by using a field line. When a dog does not respond to the whistle, the handler lets him out at quite a distance to chase the sheep. The handler then blows three times on the whistle and pulls the line so the dog is in no doubt that he must not chase sheep.

It must be remembered that all of the above takes time and patience. It is important to remember that your Dachshund is a dog – just because he is small does not mean he should be treated any differently. The Dachshund does not respond to rough handling and it can set the training back a long way if the dog is not praised and encouraged.

In order to hunt vermin, the dog must have instinct; you can then channel it correctly to give you the desired results. Running around aimlessly and accidentally flushing animals is not hunting; the Dachshund should be methodical and persistent in his hunting, using the wind to advantage and following the scent keenly.

Dachshunds are introduced to different terrains to get them used to scenting.

HINTS AND TIPS
- Ensure that your dog does not enter badger setts. Apart from the legal aspect, Dachshunds can suffer severe injuries, and possibly death, as a result of confrontation with a badger.
- Trust your dog: if he thinks there is something in a hole, there probably is; if he is disinterested, there is probably nothing there.
- Ensure any bites or cuts are thoroughly cleaned and antibiotics administered, if necessary.
- After any contact with vermin, check your dog for fleas and ticks.

FINALLY
- Remember that your dog's coat and feet are of major importance for happy, healthy hunting.
- It is crucial that he has a good undercoat that keeps him dry and warm.
- His feet should be well arched with strong pads and with thick hair for protection.
- He should have enough ground clearance to enable him to get over and through thick cover and he should be athletic enough to get into holes and turn around to get out.
- It is no good having a dog that is too fat, as this will hinder his performance and stamina.
- Exaggerations of any kind are best avoided for the working dog. Over-full fronts and too-deep chests are barriers to the dog performing the tasks he was created for and should not be viewed as desirable.

THE PERFECT DACHSHUND

Chapter 7

The Kennel Club describes a Breed Standard as: "the guideline which describes the ideal characteristics, temperament and appearance of a breed and ensures that the breed is fit for function". The introduction to every UK Breed Standard goes on to say:

"Absolute soundness is essential. Breeders and judges should at all times be careful to avoid obvious conditions or exaggerations which would be detrimental in any way to the health, welfare or soundness of this breed. From time to time certain conditions or exaggerations may be considered to have the potential to affect dogs in some breeds adversely, and judges and breeders are requested to refer to the Kennel Club website for details of any such current issues. If a feature or quality is desirable it should only be present in the right measure."

There are some important points to understand from this. When looking at a Dachshund you should always bear in mind its working origins; it should be able to do a day's work. Exaggeration of any form is to be avoided. The Dachshund is not a breed where 'more is better'. Exaggeration of size, length, lowness to ground, or too level a back can all lead to health problems, and create a dog that is not fit for its original purpose and is equally unsuitable for life today, as a family companion.

While the Breed Standard is fundamental, individual breeders' and judges' interpretations will inevitably vary and therefore opinions as to the "perfect Dachshund" will also vary. It is a blueprint – judges place different emphasis on points. This is a good thing because it is one way of avoiding everyone following a particular fashion and taking the

breed off in a totally unsuitable direction.

We are the custodians of the breed today and have a duty to protect the breed for future generations to enjoy. Most Dachshund owners say that they are owned by their dogs, and they return time and again to buy another Dachshund. Pet owners are not looking for "perfection", but a healthy, companionable dog that is easy to live with.

GOVERNING BODIES OF THE BREED STANDARD

The Dachshund has three governing bodies, each of which publishes a slightly different version of the Breed Standard. The Federation Cynologique Internationale (FCI) adopted the German Standard, as this was the country of origin of the Dachshund. This was last revised in 2001. The American Kennel Club (AKC) Standard was revised

Ch. Drakesleat Win Alot: Top winning Miniature Wire-haired Dachshund in the UK 2009/10 and Top Hound 2010.

Am. Ch. Kochana's Hiswill Ain't Misbehavin: A fine example of an American Smooth.

Int. Ch. Drakesleat Humphrey Gocart: A top winner under FCI rules.

in 2007 and the Kennel Club (KC) in the UK updated its Standard in 2009.

The latest revisions to the KC Standard were made following recommendations submitted by the Dachshund Breed Council, which represents the views of all 19 UK breed clubs. Although the three Standards are similar, there are some important differences, which go some way to explaining the different types seen in Europe, the USA and the UK. It is also worth noting that top-winning show dogs in Europe will also have had to succeed in working trials to prove their functional ability. Ireland has adopted the FCI Standard and recently established its approach to working trials. There is currently no such "formal" requirement in the USA or UK, but there is increasing interest in developing such trials as a means of keeping the Dachshund "fit for function".

INTERPRETATION AND ANALYSIS OF THE BREED STANDARDS

GENERAL APPEARANCE

KC

Moderately long and low with no exaggeration; compact, well muscled body, with enough ground clearance to allow free movement. Height at the withers should be half the length of the body, measured from breastbone to the rear of thigh. Bold, defiant carriage of head and intelligent expression.

This handsome Smooth Dachshund is bred from American lines but has proved successful in the British show ring.

AKC

Low to ground, long in body and short of leg, with robust muscular development; the skin is elastic and pliable without excessive wrinkling. Appearing neither crippled, awkward, nor cramped in his capacity for movement, the Dachshund is well balanced with bold and confident head carriage and intelligent, alert facial expression. His hunting spirit, good nose, loud tongue and distinctive build make him well-suited for below-ground work and for beating the bush. His keen nose gives him an advantage over most other breeds for trailing. NOTE: Inasmuch as the Dachshund is a hunting dog, scars from honorable wounds shall not be considered a fault.

FCI

Low, short legged, elongated but compact build, very muscular with cheeky, challenging head carriage and alert facial expression. His general appearance is typical of his sex. In spite of his legs being short in relation to the long body, he is very mobile and lithe.

With the distance above ground level of about one third of the height at withers, the body length should be in harmonious relation to height at withers, about 1 to 1.7-1.8.

The Dachshund should not be a long-backed dog; it is a short-legged dog, but one that can still cover the ground and move freely. All three Standards call for a well-muscled dog and it is clear that a dog presented in a fit, "hard" condition is preferable to one that is soft, flabby and under-exercised.

The UK Standard introduced the guidance on height to length ratio in 2009, and this is intended to avoid having dogs that are either excessively long or that are too low to the ground. Dogs that are shorter than 2:1 are to be preferred over dogs longer than this ratio. Low (to ground) means lowness from the withers, compared with other breeds, not a lack of ground clearance. There must be sufficient ground clearance to enable the dog to track over rough ground.

In comparison, the FCI Standard requires a slightly taller dog and we will see (below) that their requirement for ground clearance is also greater than in the UK.

CHARACTERISTICS AND TEMPERAMENT

KC
Intelligent, lively, courageous to the point of rashness, obedient. Especially suited to going to ground because of low build, very strong forequarters and forelegs. Long strong jaw, and immense power of bite and hold. Excellent nose, persevering hunter and tracker. Essential that functional build is retained to ensure working ability. Faithful, versatile and good tempered.

AKC
Special Characteristics of the Three Coat Varieties - The Dachshund is bred with three varieties of coat: (1) Smooth; (2) Wirehaired; (3) Longhaired and is shown in two sizes, standard and miniature. All three varieties and both sizes

Am. Can. Ch. Hundeleben Homar Aquarius: The importance of a sound temperament cannot be over-emphasised.
Pooch Photographer.

must conform to the characteristics (already) specified. The Dachshund is clever, lively and courageous to the point of rashness, persevering in above- and below-ground work, with all the senses well developed. Any display of shyness is a serious fault.

FCI
Friendly by nature, neither nervous nor aggressive, with even temperament. Passionate, persevering and fast hunting dog with an excellent nose.

All three Standards emphasise the fact that Dachshunds should be good tempered, bold and outgoing. Given that the "function" of the majority of Dachshunds today is to be family pets, temperament has to be one of the most important considerations of any breeder. Nervous dogs are no fun to live with, and they cannot be living fulfilled lives themselves if they are forever worried or stressed by things they come across in their daily routine. In the show ring, dogs that are nervous or aggressive should be seriously penalised by judges.

A tail held low, between the legs, suggests a dog is nervous and his temperament may lead him to fear-biting, which is potentially very dangerous for anyone meeting that dog. Nervous dogs are usually easy to spot, as they will tend to scuttle along on the lead, ears held back, and often they will be panting with fear.

When out and about, and coming across new dogs, some Dachshunds can be a bit 'breed-ist' and appear rather aggressive towards bigger dogs; more so when they are on the lead than

DIFFERENT HEAD TYPES

The head of the Smooth (left), Long (centre) and Wire (right) all share the same conical shape, but the Wire's skull appears slightly broader.

when running loose. Generally, they will bark first and ask questions later, but it is unusual for a Dachshund to be truly aggressive towards another dog. Presumably, if you were that small and low to ground, everything else would seem rather large and potentially threatening, so you might want to assert yourself first!

HEAD AND SKULL

KC

Long, appearing conical when seen from above; from side tapering uniformly to tip of nose. Skull only slightly arched. Neither too broad nor too narrow, sloping gradually without prominent stop into slightly arched muzzle. Length from tip of nose to eyes equal to length from eyes to occiput. In Wire haired, particularly, ridges over eyes strongly prominent, giving appearance of slightly broader skull. Lips well stretched, neatly covering lower jaw. Strong jaw bones not too square or snipy, but opening wide.

AKC

Viewed from above or from the side, the head tapers uniformly to the tip of the nose. The eyes are of medium size, almond-shaped and dark-rimmed, with an energetic, pleasant expression; not piercing; very dark in color. The bridge bones over the eyes are strongly prominent. The skull is slightly arched, neither too broad nor too narrow, and slopes gradually with little perceptible stop into the finely-formed, slightly arched muzzle, giving a Roman appearance. Lips are tightly stretched, well covering the lower jaw. Nostrils well open. Jaws opening wide and hinged well back of the eyes, with strongly developed bones and teeth.

FCI

Elongated as seen from above and in profile. Tapering uniformly towards the nose leather yet not pointed. Superciliary ridges clearly defined. Nasal cartilage and bridge of nose, long and narrow.

CRANIAL REGION:
Skull: Rather flat, gradually merging with the slightly arched nasal bridge.
Stop: Only indicated.

FACIAL REGION:
Nose: Leather well developed.
Muzzle: Long, sufficiently broad and strong. Can be opened wide, split to level of eye.
Lips: Taut fitting, covering the lower jaw well.

The head of a male Dachshund will obviously look stronger than that of a bitch, but both should be the same conical shape when viewed from above. Unlike the judging of some other breeds, the Dachshund is not considered to be a "head breed" and its appearance is far less important in the overall scheme of things. However, a very domed head and low-set ears will radically alter the otherwise pleasing appearance of a good head.

There should be no pronounced "stop" between the skull and the muzzle and the distance from the back of the skull to the eyes should be the same length as from the eyes to the tip of the nose. A Roman nose is to be preferred and greatly adds to the general intelligent

The typical Dachshund expression comes from almond-shaped eyes and mobile ears.

appearance of the Dachshund.

The Dachshund's jaws should be powerful; remember his working origins where he was required to go to ground and to hold prey.

EYES

KC
Medium size, almond-shaped, set obliquely. Dark except in Chocolates, where they can be lighter. In Dapples, one or both 'wall' eyes permissible.

AKC
Wall eyes, except in the case of dappled dogs, are a serious fault.

FCI
Medium size, oval, set well apart, with clear energetic yet friendly expression. Not piercing.

Colour bright, dark reddish brown to blackish brown in all coat colours. Wall, fish or pearl eyes in dapple dogs are not desired but may be tolerated.

An almond-shaped, dark eye is a major factor in giving a Dachshund his desired expression. Round eyes make him look like a toy dog, and light eyes can make him look staring and aggressive (although he probably is not). A round eye is more likely to be seen in the Miniature varieties and when combined with a domed skull and short muzzle really does make for a non-typical "toy-ish" head.

Chocolate and Tan Dachshunds usually have lighter-coloured eyes and, when combined with quite pink eye-rims, their expression is not to everyone's taste.

EARS

KC
Set high, and not too far forward. Broad, of moderate length and well rounded (not pointed or folded). Forward edge touching cheek. Mobile, and when at attention back of ear directed forward and outward.

AKC

The ears are set near the top of the head, not too far forward, of moderate length, rounded, not narrow, pointed, or folded. Their carriage, when animated, is with the forward edge just touching the cheek so that the ears frame the face.

FCI

Set on high, not too far forward. Sufficiently long but not exaggerated. Rounded, not narrow, pointed or folded. Mobile with front edge lying close to cheek.

The Dachshund's ears are quite expressive and when he is 'at attention' should stand out from the head, but with the front edge still touching the cheek. If you pull the ear forward, it should come to about halfway between the eye and the tip of the nose. Ears that are too small will make him look like a terrier and they should certainly not be pricked.

The ear leather should not be fine; again, remember his working origins where a fine ear would have been easily torn by his prey or by the undergrowth through which the Dachshund works.

Long-haired Dachshunds should be well feathered on the outside of the ears, with the hair falling below the bottom of the ear. Wires should have relatively smooth ears and certainly no feathering.

The teeth are strongly developed and should meet in a scissor bite with the upper teeth closely overlapping the lower teeth.

MOUTH

KC

Teeth strongly developed, powerful canine teeth fitting closely. Jaws strong, with a perfect, regular and complete scissor bite, i.e. upper teeth closely overlapping lower teeth and set square to the jaws. Complete dentition important.

AKC

Powerful canine teeth; teeth fit closely together in a scissors bite. An even bite is a minor fault. Any other deviation is a serious fault.

FCI

Well developed upper and lower jaw. Scissor bite, even and closing firmly. Ideally, complete set of 42 teeth according to requirements for a dog's mouth with strong canines exactly fitting into each other.

The correct mouth should be a scissor bite, with closely fitting top and bottom canine teeth. Any deviation from this is a fault: for example, an overshot jaw, where the top teeth overlap the bottom teeth by a significant margin, or an undershot jaw, where the top teeth close behind the lower canines. An overshot jaw is more common than an undershot jaw. Neither of these faults is likely to be a problem for a Dachshund living as a pet, but he would not be able to grasp and hold his prey firmly if he was a working dog with either of these faults.

Occasionally, you may come across a pincer bite, where both upper and lower teeth meet exactly edge to edge. This, too, is incorrect.

Complete dentition means there should be 22 lower teeth and 20 upper teeth. There should be six incisors in each jaw. Occasionally, one incisor might be missing, but occasionally two are missing; both situations are faults. There should be two canines in each jaw – one on each side. There should be eight pre-molars in each jaw – four on each side; missing pre-molars would also be considered to be faulty. There should be four molars in the upper jaw – two on each side – and six in the lower jaw – three on each side.

A full set of teeth means the dog can grip strongly; if you try to prise a Dachshund's jaws apart, you should be able to feel how powerful his jaws are. This applies as much in the Miniatures as the Standards; they should not have soft, toy-ish mouths or weak jaws.

NECK

KC

Long, muscular, clean with no dewlap, slightly arched, running in graceful lines into shoulders, carried proudly forward.

It is important that exaggeration does not creep into the front assembly; ground clearance is essential.

AKC

Long, muscular, clean-cut, without dewlap, slightly arched in the nape, flowing gracefully into the shoulders without creating the impression of a right angle.

FCI

Sufficiently long, muscular. Tight fitting skin on throat. Lightly arched nape of neck, carried freely and high.

The Dachshund's length of neck provides his defiant head carriage; he should look elegant and the neck should flow smoothly into the withers. There should not be a sharp, angular change from the neck into the withers; this will often be associated with upright shoulder placement.

A short neck gives a stuffy appearance which completely spoils the overall balance of the dog. Short, stuffy necks are more commonly seen in Miniature Long-haired Dachshunds, where they can appear even more stuffy if the dog has a particularly profuse coat.

The skin should fit closely all over the body, including the neck, where there should be no dewlap (baggy skin under the neck).

FOREQUARTERS

KC

Shoulder blades long, broad, and placed firmly and obliquely (45 degrees to the horizontal) upon very robust rib cage. Upper arm the same length as shoulder blade, set at 90 degrees

to it, very strong, and covered with hard, supple muscles. Upper arm lies close to ribs, but able to move freely. Forearm short and strong in bone, inclining slightly inwards; when seen in profile moderately straight, must not bend forward or knuckle over, which indicates unsoundness. Correctly placed foreleg should cover the lowest point of the keel.

AKC

For effective underground work, the front must be strong, deep, long and cleanly muscled. Forequarters in detail:
Chest – The breast-bone is strongly prominent in front so that on either side a depression or dimple appears. When viewed from the front, the thorax appears oval and extends downward to the mid-point of the forearm. The enclosing structure of the well-sprung ribs appears full and oval to allow, by its ample capacity, complete development of heart and lungs. The keel merges gradually into the line of the abdomen and extends well beyond the front legs. Viewed in profile, the lowest point of the breast line is covered by the front leg.
Shoulder blades – Long, broad, well laid back and firmly placed upon the fully developed thorax, closely fitted at the withers, furnished with hard yet pliable muscles.
Upper Arm – Ideally the same length as the shoulder blade and at right angles to the latter, strong of bone and hard of

muscle, lying close to the ribs, with elbows close to the body, yet capable of free movement. Forearm – Short; supplied with hard yet pliable muscles on the front and outside, with tightly stretched tendons on the inside and at the back, slightly curved inwards. The joints between the forearms and the feet (wrists) are closer together than the shoulder joints, so that the front does not appear absolutely straight. The inclined shoulder blades, upper arms and curved forearms form parentheses that enclose the ribcage, creating the correct "wraparound front." Knuckling over is a disqualifying fault.

FCI

General: Strongly muscled, well angulated. Seen from front, clean front legs, standing straight with good strength of bone; feet pointing straight forward.
Shoulders: Pliant muscles. Long sloping shoulder blade, fitting close to chest.
Upper arm: Equal in length to shoulder blade, set almost at right angle to same. Strong boned and well muscled, close fitting to ribs but free in movement.
Elbows: Turning neither in nor out.
Forearm: Short, yet so long that the dog's distance from the ground is about one third of its height at withers. As straight as possible.
Pastern joints: Slightly closer together than the shoulder

joints.
Pastern: Seen from the side, should be neither steep nor noticeably inclined forward.

All three Standards devote considerable space to the definition of the front of a Dachshund, which is one of his defining characteristics. The AKC Standard is particularly explicit, with its description of angles and lengths, and really requires little further explanation.

The Dachshund's front is one area where exaggeration can creep in, but it really is a case of 'more is definitely not better'. A very deep chest is a fault, as insufficient ground clearance will restrict the dog's movement and ability to do a day's work. At its lowest point, between the forelegs, it should be approximately half way between the elbow and the wrist (knee). Judges should not be afraid to reward dogs showing greater ground clearance than this.

"Low to ground" means

lowness from the withers, not lack of ground clearance. The height from withers to the bottom of the keel should be approximately 75 per cent of the total height from withers to the ground. Under the FCI Standard, the preferred ratio is two-thirds body depth to one-third ground clearance.

The point of the breastbone should be prominent and high up (rather like looking at the bow of a ship). A flat or 'terrier' front will often be associated with upright shoulder placement and a short upper arm.

When you look at a Dachshund from the front, his forelegs should fit closely to his forechest and his elbows should not stick out like chicken wings.

BODY

KC

Moderately long and full muscled. Sloping shoulders, back reasonably level, blending harmoniously between withers

The length of the body is moderately long with a short, strong loin.

and slightly arched loin. Loin short and strong. Breast bone strong, and so prominent that a depression appears on either side of it in front. When viewed from front, thorax full and oval; when viewed from side or above, full volumed, so allowing by its ample capacity complete development of heart and lungs. Well ribbed up, underline gradually merging into line of abdomen. Body sufficiently clear of ground to allow free movement.

AKC

The trunk is long and fully muscled. When viewed in profile, the back lies in the straightest possible line between the withers and the short, very slightly arched loin. A body that hangs loosely between the shoulders is a serious fault.
Abdomen – Slightly drawn up.

FCI

Upper line: Blending harmoniously from neck to slightly sloping croup.
Withers: Pronounced.
Back: Behind the high withers, topline running from the thoracic vertebrae straight or slightly inclined to the rear. Firm and well muscled.
Loins: Strongly muscled. Sufficiently long.
Croup: Broad and sufficiently long. Slightly sloping.
Chest: Sternum well developed and so prominent that slight depressions appear on either side. The ribcage, seen from the

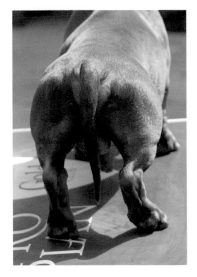

The hindquarters should be well angulated and powerful.

front, is oval. Seen from above and the side, it is roomy, giving plenty of space for the heart and lung development. Ribs carried well back. With correct length and angulation of shoulder blade and upper arm, the front leg covers the lowest point of the sternal line in profile.
Underline and Belly: Slight tuck up.
Skin: Tight fitting.

The Dachshund's length should not be exaggerated. His length is in the body and not the back. Ribs should go well back and loin should be short, to give strength. Too long a dog may result in a weak back, with associated health risks. Too short a body gives a cloddy appearance.

The line of the back from

withers to rump should be reasonably level. There should be a slight rise to the loin, but this does not mean roach-backed. A 'dead flat' topline is not what is required, nor is a hollow back, sometimes known as 'soft in back'.

The underline should not be tucked up to the abdomen (like a Greyhound), which can give the appearance of the dog being too thin. The body should be muscular and should feel in 'hard' condition when you put your hands on. The body should not be 'rolling in fat', which is a clear sign that the dog is either over-fed, under-exercised, or a combination of both.

HINDQUARTERS

KC

Rump full, broad and strong, pliant muscles. Croup long, full, robustly muscled, only slightly sloping towards tail. Pelvis strong, set obliquely and not too short. Upper thigh set at right angles to pelvis, strong and of good length. Lower thigh short, set at right angles to upper thigh and well muscled. Legs when seen behind set well apart, straight, and parallel.

AKC

Strong and cleanly muscled. The pelvis, the thigh, the second thigh, and the rear pastern are ideally the same length and give the appearance of a series of right angles. From the rear, the thighs are strong and powerful. The legs turn neither in nor out.

Rear pasterns – Short and strong, perpendicular to the second thigh bone. When viewed from behind, they are upright and parallel.

Feet – Hind paws – Smaller than the front paws with four compactly closed and arched toes with tough, thick pads. The entire foot points straight ahead and is balanced equally on the ball and not merely on the toes. Rear dewclaws should be removed.

Croup – Long, rounded and full, sinking slightly towards the tail.

FCI

General: Strongly muscled, in correct proportion to forequarters. Strong angulation of stifles and hock joints. Hindlegs parallel standing neither close nor wide apart.

Upper thigh: Should be of good length and well muscled.

Stifle (joint): Broad and strong with pronounced angulation.

Lower thigh: Short, almost at right angle to upper thigh. Well muscled.

Hock joint: Clean with strong tendons.

Hock: Relatively long, mobile towards lower thigh. Lightly curved forward.

The hindquarters provide the drive of the Dachshund when moving and therefore a well-angulated hind end is essential. The KC Standard clearly specifies the pelvis, upper thigh and lower thigh should be set at a series of right-angles, while the AKC Standard also advises that each of these bones should be of equal length.

In the current version of the KC Standard, the lower thigh is described as "short", which sometimes causes confusion. In an earlier KC Standard, the phrase was "short in comparison with other animals", which was a reminder that the Dachshund is a short-legged breed. If the lower thigh is shorter than the pelvis and upper thigh, it is likely that the dog would move with very cramped movement. When viewed in profile, the hock joint should stand out just behind the dog's rump and you should be able to place a vertical hand against the rump, supported on the hock joint. An over-angulated hind end will lead to unsound, wobbly movement.

Dachshund exhibitors often use the term "hock" to refer to the whole length of the bones from the hock joint to the feet. Strictly speaking, the hock is simply the joint between the lower thigh and the foot bones and corresponds to the ankle in humans. In the Dachshund, when standing, the bones from the hock to the ground should be perpendicular to the ground (i.e. not tucked under the body, which is a sign of an incorrectly angulated and weak back end).

When viewed from behind, the hind legs should be perfectly parallel to each other. If the hock joints are turned in towards each other, this is described as 'cow-hocked' and if they turn outwards, it is described as 'bandy-hocked'.

Both of these are faulty construction and are likely to be backed up with incorrect movement when you watch the dog moving away from you. Some dogs may appear slightly cow-hocked when stood still, but are perfectly parallel (correct) when moving away. The rump, viewed from behind, should be broad and muscular, with the legs set well apart, otherwise the dog will be seen to move 'close behind' when walking away from you.

FEET

KC
Front feet full, broad, deep, close knit, straight or very

Dachshunds are great diggers, and this is reflected in their broad, well-arched front feet.

slightly turned out. Hindfeet smaller and narrower. Toes close together, with a decided arch to each toe, strong regularly placed nails, thick and firm pads. Dog must stand true, i.e. equally on all parts of the foot.

AKC

Front paws are full, tight, compact, with well-arched toes and tough, thick pads. They may be equally inclined a trifle outward. There are five toes, four in use, close together with a pronounced arch and strong, short nails. Front dewclaws may be removed.

FCI

Front feet: Toes close together, well arched with strong, resistant, well cushioned pads and short strong nails. The fifth toe has no function but must not be removed.
Hind feet: Four close knit toes, well arched. Standing firmly on strong pads.

Anyone who owns a Dachshund will know they are great diggers. For that, they need broad, well-arched front feet, with strong toes and tough pads. Neither a small, round "terrier foot", nor a long, thin "hare foot" are correct. A dog that is insufficiently exercised will have soft pads and may also be down on its pasterns (and appear to be flat-footed).

When viewed from the front, the feet should ideally be pointing straight ahead, or only slightly turned outwards ('five to one', not 'ten to two').

The skin on the front legs should be tight-fitting, not wrinkled. Loose, wrinkled skin is at risk of being torn when the dog is out working in rough undergrowth.

Dewclaws will be present on front feet and maybe also on hind feet. The KC Standard no longer refers to the removal of dewclaws and it can be seen that the AKC and FCI Standards are not in agreement on removal of these. Certainly in the UK, many veterinary surgeons will no longer agree to remove dewclaws from newborn puppies, presumably seeing this as a form of mutilation similar to tail docking.

TAIL

KC

Continues line of the spine, but slightly curved, without kinks or twists, not carried too high, or touching ground when at rest.

AKC

Set in continuation of the spine, extending without kinks, twists, or pronounced curvature, and not carried too gaily.

FCI

Not set on too high, carried in continuation of topline. A slight curve in the last third of the tail is permitted.

We do not want a tail set on high; it should be an extension of the topline. Neither should it be

held high like a Beagle, as this spoils the Dachshund's overall appearance of length and balance. A happy dog with a high-set tail will wag his tail in an upright position instead of from side to side. An ill-tempered dog will also tend to hold his tail high and quivering, as a sign of aggression to other dogs. A nervous dog will have his tail held low, clamped between his hind legs.

The texture and length of hair on the tail is described below (under Coat).

GAIT/MOVEMENT

KC

Should be free and flowing. Stride should be long, with the drive coming from the hindquarters when viewed from the side. Viewed from in front or behind, the legs and feet should move parallel to each other with the distance apart being the width of the shoulder and hip joints respectively.

AKC

Fluid and smooth. Forelegs reach well forward, without much lift, in unison with the driving action of hind legs. The correct shoulder assembly and well-fitted elbows allow the long, free stride in front. Viewed from the front, the legs do not move in exact parallel planes, but incline slightly inward. Hind legs drive on a line with the forelegs, with hock joints and rear pasterns (metatarsus) turning neither in nor out. The

-Movement should be energetic with far-reaching front strides.

propulsion of the hind leg depends on the dog's ability to carry the hind leg to complete extension. Viewed in profile, the forward reach of the hind leg equals the rear extension. The thrust of correct movement is seen when the rear pads are clearly exposed during rear extension. Rear feet do not reach upward toward the abdomen and there is no appearance of walking on the rear pasterns. Feet must travel parallel to the line of motion with no tendency to swing out, cross over, or interfere with each other. Short, choppy movement, rolling or high-stepping gait, close or overly wide coming or going are incorrect. The Dachshund must have agility, freedom of movement, and endurance to do the work for which he was developed.

FCI
Movement should be ground covering, flowing and energetic, with far reaching front strides without much lift, and strong rear drive movement should produce slightly springy transmission to backline. Tail should be carried in harmonious continuation of backline, slightly sloping. Front and hindlegs have parallel movement.

Once again, the AKC Standard is much more explicit and helpful in its description of the Dachshund's movement. When

he is coming towards you, his front legs should appear parallel, not paddling outwards, or excessively crooked inwards. Moving away, his hind legs should be parallel and you should be able to see the pads of his rear feet as he extends his legs backwards.

In profile, his front legs should extend well out as he reaches forward and then extend well back under his body. A short, stilted gait is a sign of a short upper arm and straight shoulder. Equally, we do not want a high-lifting goose-step or 'hackneyed' movement of the forelegs.

The hind legs, in profile, must also reach well forward and equally far behind. As with the front movement, a short, restricted or stilted gait is a sign of incorrect angulation, caused by short pelvic and thigh bones. Some Dachshunds with too steep a pelvis and excessive length of metatarsals will stand sickle-

hocked and are likely to move in a so-called 'tummy-tapping' motion. Here, there is no rear extension and the dog appears to be moving with its hind legs tucked under its body, almost touching its stomach on the forward extension.

COAT: SMOOTH-HAIRED

KC
Dense, short and smooth. Hair on underside of tail coarse in texture. Skin loose and supple, but fitting closely all over without dewlap and little or no wrinkle.

AKC
Short, smooth and shining. Should be neither too long nor too thick. Ears not leathery. Tail - Gradually tapered to a point, well but not too richly haired. Long sleek bristles on the underside are considered a patch of strong-growing hair,

The Smooth coat is short, dense and shiny.

The Long coat is soft, and although there is abundant feathering it should not obscure the outline.

not a fault. A brush tail is a fault, as is also a partly or wholly hairless tail.

FCI

Short, dense, shiny, smooth fitting, tight and harsh. Not showing any bald patches anywhere.
Tail: Fine, fully but not too profusely coated. Somewhat longer guard hair on underside is not a fault.

COAT: LONG-HAIRED

KC

Soft and straight, or only slightly waved; longest under neck, on underparts of body and behind legs, where it forms abundant feathering, on tail where it forms a flag. Outside of ears well feathered. Coat flat and not obscuring outline. Too much hair on feet undesirable.

AKC

The sleek, glistening, often slightly wavy hair is longer under the neck and on forechest, the underside of the body, the ears and behind the legs. The coat gives the dog an elegant appearance. Short hair on the ear is not desirable. Too profuse a coat which masks type, equally long hair over the whole body, a curly coat, or a pronounced parting on the back are faults.
Tail – Carried gracefully in prolongation of the spine; the hair attains its greatest length here and forms a veritable flag.

FCI

The sleek shiny coat, with undercoat and close fitting to body, is longer at the throat and on underside of body. On leathers the hair must extend beyond the lower edge of ears (feathering). Distinct feathers

on rear side of legs. Achieves its greatest length on underside of tail and there forms a veritable flag.

COAT: WIRE-HAIRED

KC

With exception of jaw, eyebrows, chin and ears, the whole body should be covered with a short, straight, harsh coat with dense undercoat, beard on the chin, eyebrows bushy, but hair on ears almost smooth. Legs and feet well but neatly furnished with harsh coat.

AKC

With the exception of jaw, eyebrows, and ears, the whole body is covered with a uniform tight, short, thick, rough, hard, outer coat but with finer, somewhat softer, shorter hairs (undercoat) everywhere distributed between the coarser

The Wire coat is short, straight and harsh, with the exception of the head furnishings.

hairs. The absence of an undercoat is a fault. The distinctive facial furnishings include a beard and eyebrows. On the ears the hair is shorter than on the body, almost smooth. The general arrangement of the hair is such that the wirehaired Dachshund, when viewed from a distance, resembles the smooth. Any sort of soft hair in the outercoat, wherever found on the body, especially on the top of the head, is a fault. The same is true of long, curly, or wavy hair, or hair that sticks out irregularly in all directions. Tail – Robust, thickly haired, gradually tapering to a point. A flag tail is a fault.

FCI
HAIR: With exception of muzzle, eyebrows and leathers, perfectly even close fitting, dense wiry topcoat with

undercoat. The muzzle has a clearly defined beard. Eyebrows are bushy. On the leathers, the coat is shorter than on the body, almost smooth.
Tail: Well and evenly covered with close fitting coat.

All three Standards are very clear on the requirements for each of the three types of coat and we've already described them in an earlier chapter. A Smooth in top condition should have a gleaming coat. A Long will not have an excessive or fluffy coat that makes it look like an animated floor mop when on the move. A Wire should have a rough coat, suited to his working role; he should not be a fluffy, trimmed dog.

COLOUR

KC
All colours permitted but no white permissible, save for a

small patch on chest which is permitted but not desirable. The dapple pattern is expressed as lighter coloured areas contrasting with the darker base. Neither the light nor the dark colour should predominate. Double dapple (where varying amounts of white occurs all over the body in addition to the dapple pattern) is unacceptable. Nose and nails black in all colours except chocolate/tan and chocolate/dapple where they are brown.

AKC
Smooth and Long-haired: Although base color is immaterial, certain patterns and basic colors predominate. One-colored Dachshunds include red and cream, with or without a shading of interspersed dark hairs. A small amount of white on the chest is acceptable, but

not desirable. Nose and nails – black. Two-colored Dachshunds include black, chocolate, wild boar, gray (blue) and fawn (Isabella), each with deep, rich tan or cream markings over the eyes, on the sides of the jaw and underlip, on the inner edge of the ear, front, breast, sometimes on the throat, inside and behind the front legs, on the paws and around the anus, and

A Miniature Dachshund being weighed before judging in the UK.

from there to about one-third to one-half of the length of the tail on the underside. Undue prominence of tan or cream markings is undesirable. A small amount of white on the chest is acceptable but not desirable. Nose and nails – in the case of black dogs, black; for chocolate and all other colors, dark brown, but self-colored is acceptable. Dappled Dachshunds – The dapple (merle) pattern is expressed as lighter-colored areas contrasting with the darker base color, which may be any acceptable color. Neither the light nor the dark color should predominate. Nose and nails are the same as for one- and two-colored Dachshunds. Partial or wholly blue (wall) eyes are as acceptable as dark eyes. A large area of white on the chest of a dapple is permissible.

Brindle is a pattern (as opposed to a color) in which black or dark stripes occur over the entire body although in some specimens the pattern may be visible only in the tan points.

Sable – The sable pattern consists of a uniform dark overlay on red dogs. The overlay hairs are double-pigmented, with the tip of each hair much darker than the base color. The pattern usually displays a widow's peak on the head. Nose, nails and eye rims are black. Eyes are dark, the darker the better.

Wire-haired: While the most common colors are wild boar, black and tan, and various shades of red, all colors and patterns listed above are admissible.

Wild boar (agouti) appears as banding of the individual hairs and imparts an overall grizzled effect which is most often seen on wirehaired Dachshunds, but may also appear on other coats. Tan points may or may not be evident. Variations include red boar and chocolate-and-tan boar. Nose, nails and eye rims are black on wild-boar and red-boar Dachshunds. On chocolate-and-tan-boar Dachshunds, nose, nails, eye rims and eyes are self-colored, the darker the better. A small amount of white on the chest, although acceptable, is not desirable. Nose and nails – same as for the smooth variety.

FCI

Smooth and Long-haired:
a) Whole-coloured: Red, reddish yellow, yellow, all with or without interspersed black hairs. A clear colour is preferable and red is of greater value than reddish yellow or yellow.

Even dogs with strongly interspersed black hairs are classed as whole-colour, not as other colours. White is not desired but single small spots do not disqualify. Nose and nails black. Reddish-brown is also permissible but not desirable.

b) Two-coloured: Deep black or brown, each with tan or yellow markings over eyes, on sides of muzzle and of lower lip, on inner edge of leathers, on forechest, on inside and rear side of legs, also on the feet, round the vent and from there reaching to about one-third or one-half of the underside of the tail. Nose and nails black in black dogs, brown in brown dogs. White is not desired but single small spots do not disqualify. Tan or yellow marking too widespread is undesirable.

c) Dappled (tiger-brindle, brindle): The basic colour is always the dark colour (black, red or grey). Desired are irregular grey or beige patches (large patches not desired). Neither the dark nor the light colour should be predominant. The colour of a brindle Dachshund is red or yellow with darker brindle. Nose and toenails are the same as with the whole- and two-coloured. Wire-haired: Dominantly light to dark wild boar colour as well as colour of dry leaves. Otherwise same colours as described under Smooth-haired a-c.

Dachshunds come in a multitude of colours so there is

The judge must decide which dog, in their opinion, conforms most closely to the Breed Standard.

something to suit everyone. However, dogs with large patches of white are not acceptable, for example 'piebald'. There are potentially lethal health risks associated with mating two dapples together. So-called 'double dapples' are at risk of being born blind and/or deaf and, because of this, the KC will no longer register puppies born from two dapple parents.

Dachshund buyers should not be taken in by adverts claiming to have rare colours for sale. This is usually a sign of a backyard breeder, or puppy farmer, who does not understand the Breed Standard or have the welfare of Dachshunds as their prime concern.

SIZE

KC
Ideal weight: 9-12 kgs (20-26 lbs).

Miniature ideal weight: 4.5kgs (10lbs). Desired maximum weight 5kgs (11lbs). Exhibits which appear thin and undernourished should be severely penalised.

AKC
Bred and shown in two sizes, standard and miniature; miniatures are not a separate classification but compete in a class division for "11 pounds and under at 12 months of age and older." Weight of the standard size is usually between 16 and 32 pounds.

FCI
Dachshund: Circumference of chest 35 cm. Upper weight limit about 9 kg.
Miniature Dachshund: Circumference of chest from 30 to 35 cm measured when at least 15 months old.
Rabbit Dachshund: Chest circumference up to 30 cm measured when at least 15 months.
Weight: Standard Dachshund up to about 9 kg.

In the UK, Miniature Dachshunds may be weighed by judges to determine their size compared with the ideal given in the Standard. Countless breeders have shown, over 60 years, that it

FAULTS

KC

Any departure from the foregoing points, including desired body condition, should be considered a fault and the seriousness with which the fault should be regarded should be in exact proportion to its degree and its effect upon the health and welfare of the dog.

Note

Male animals should have two apparently normal testicles fully descended into the scrotum.

AKC

The foregoing description is that of the ideal Dachshund. Any deviation from the above described dog must be penalized to the extent of the deviation keeping in mind the importance of the contribution of the various features toward the basic original purpose of the breed.

DISQUALIFICATION: Knuckling over of front legs.

FCI

Any departure from the foregoing points should be considered a fault and the seriousness with which the fault should be regarded should be in exact proportion to its degree and its effect upon the health and welfare of the dog.

M3 (Molar 3) are not to be considered when judging. Lack of 2PM1 (Premolar 1) is not to be penalised. The absence of PM2 should be regarded as a fault, if other than M3, no other teeth are missing, also a departure from the correctly closing scissor bite.

SERIOUS FAULTS:

Weak, long-legged or body trailing on ground.
The absence of teeth other than those described among Faults or Eliminating faults.
Wall eye in any colour other than dapple.
Pointed, very folded ear leathers.
Body suspended between shoulders.
Hollow back, roach back.
Weak loins.
Marked running up at rear (croup higher than withers).
Chest too weak.
Flanks with whippety-like tuck up.
Badly angulated fore- and hindquarters.
Narrow hindquarters, lacking muscle.
Cow hocks or bow legs.
Feet turning markedly inwards or outwards.
Splayed toes.
Heavy, clumsy, waddling movement.

---

is possible to breed fit and healthy Miniature Dachshunds that do not exceed 5 kg/11 lbs. Experience outside the UK has shown that, without a means of ensuring Miniatures fall within the 5 kg/11 lbs desired maximum weight, it is inevitable that their size will increase and they will become indistinguishable from the smaller specimens of Standard Dachshunds.

Under FCI rules, Dachshunds are measured for their chest circumference, rather than being weighed to determine which variety they are. Interestingly, the Deutscher Teckel Club recognised that the size of Standard Dachshunds was increasing beyond the desired maximum and introduced weighing to help avoid exaggeration. There is also discussion in the UK about the

excessive size of some Standard Dachshunds, well above the 20-26 lbs. (9-12 kgs) ideal weight. Such large dogs are far removed from their working origins and many would struggle to do a day's work.

It is essential we all strive to keep the Dachshund (Miniature and Standard) within the ideal sizes specified in the Breed Standard. While a larger dog might look impressive, you have to

FAULTY COAT:

SMOOTH-HAIRED DACHSHUND:
Coat too fine or thin. Bald patches on leathers (leather ear), other bald areas.
Coat much too coarse and much too profuse.
Brush like tail.
Tail partially or wholly hairless.
Black colour without any marking (Brand).

WIRE-HAIRED DACHSHUND:
Soft coat, whether long or short.
Long coat, standing away from body in all directions.
Curly or wavy coat.
Soft coat on head.
Flag on tail.
Lack of beard.
Lack of undercoat.
Short coat.

LONG-HAIRED DACHSHUND:
Coat of equal length all over body.
Wavy or shaggy coat.
Lack of flag (tail).
Lack of overhanging feathering on ears.

Short coat.
Pronounced parting in coat on back.
Hair too long between toes.

ELIMINATING FAULTS:
Very anxious or aggressive nature.
Overshot or undershot mouth, wry mouth.
Faulty position of the lower canines.
Absence of one or more canines; absence of one or more incisors.
Lack of other premolars or molars.
Exceptions: The two PM1, one PM2 without consideration of M3, as mentioned under Faults.
Chest: Sternum cut off.
Any fault of tail.
Very loose shoulders.
Knuckling over in pasterns.
Black colour without markings; white colour with or without markings.
Colours other than those listed under "Colour".

Any dog clearly showing physical or behavioural abnormalities shall be disqualified.

Male animals should have two apparently normal testicles fully descended into the scrotum.

remember the Dachshund's original purpose. For the majority of Dachshunds living life as a pet, if an owner wants a Miniature Dachshund, they want one that is portable and not a 'small Standard'. Similarly, buyers of Standards do not want a dog of 30-40 lbs (14-18 kgs) in weight that they cannot easily lift in and out of their car, or put on to a table at home for grooming.

SUMMARY
The Breed Standard paints a picture of the 'perfect Dachshund', but most of us have yet to see one! If you decide to breed, it is also essential to use the most suitable dog on your bitch (conformation, temperament and bloodlines that complement your bitch), not just the latest Champion or winning dog in the show ring. Winners do

not always breed winners. Good luck in your quest for perfection. The Standard is something for breeders to strive for, but at all times bearing in mind the importance of health, welfare, temperament, and the avoidance of exaggeration.

In reality, however your Dachshund compares with the Standard, we are sure that, to you, he is the 'perfect Dachshund'.

HAPPY AND HEALTHY

Chapter 8

The six varieties of Dachshund are stoical dogs with a lifespan that can run into double figures, especially among Miniatures. The Dachshund is renowned as a faithful companion and a willing friend on a non-conditional basis. He will, however, of necessity rely on you for food and shelter, accident prevention and medication. A healthy Dachshund is a happy chap, looking to please and amuse his owner.

There are a few genetic conditions recognised in the six varieties of Dachshund, which will be covered later in the chapter.

VACCINATION
There is much debate over the issue of vaccination at the moment. The timing of the final part of the initial vaccination course for a puppy and the frequency of subsequent booster vaccinations are both under scrutiny. An evaluation of the relative risk for each disease plays a part, depending on the local situation.

Many owners think that the actual vaccination is the protection, so that their puppy can go out for walks as soon as he has had the final part of the puppy vaccination course. This is not the case. The rationale behind vaccination is to stimulate the immune system into producing protective antibodies, which will be triggered if the dog is subsequently exposed to that particular disease. This means that a further one or two weeks will have to pass before an effective level of protection will have developed.

Vaccines against viruses stimulate longer-lasting protection than those against bacteria, whose effect may only persist for a matter of months, in some cases. There is also the possibility of an individual failing to mount a full immune response to a vaccination: although the vaccine schedule may have been followed as recommended, that particular dog remains vulnerable.

It is worth remembering that maintaining a fully effective level of immune protection against the disease appropriate to your locale is vital: these are serious diseases, which may result in the death of your dog, and some may have the potential to be passed on to his human family (so-called zoonotic potential for transmission). This is where you will be grateful for your veterinary surgeon's own knowledge and advice.

A dog's level of protection against rabies, as demonstrated by the antibody titre in a blood sample, is routinely tested in the UK in order to fulfil the requirements of the Pet Travel

Scheme (PETS).

This is not required at the current time with any other individual diseases in order to gauge the need for booster vaccination or to determine the effect of a course of vaccines. Instead, your veterinary surgeon will advise a protocol based upon the vaccines available, local disease prevalence, and the lifestyle of you and your dog.

The American Animal Hospital Association laid down guidance at the end of 2006 for the vaccination of dogs in North America. Core diseases were defined as distemper, adenovirus, parvovirus and rabies. So-called non-core diseases are kennel cough, Lyme disease and leptospirosis. A decision to vaccinate against one or more non-core diseases will be based on an individual's level of risk, determined by lifestyle and where you live.

Remember, however, that the booster visit to the veterinary surgery is not 'just' for a booster. I am regularly correcting my clients when they announce that they have 'just' brought their pet for a booster. Instead, this appointment is a chance for a full healthcheck and evaluation of how a particular dog is doing. After all, we are all conversant with the adage that a human year is equivalent to seven canine years. There have been attempts in recent times to reset the scale for two reasons: small breeds live longer than giant breeds, and dogs are living longer than previously. I have seen dogs of 17 and 18 years of age, but to say a dog is 119 or 126 years old is plainly meaningless. A dog's health can change dramatically over the course of a single year, because dogs age at a far faster rate than humans.

For me as a veterinary surgeon,

the booster vaccination visit is a challenge: how much can I find of which the owner was unaware, such as rotten teeth or a heart murmur? Even monitoring bodyweight year upon year is of use, because bodyweight can creep up, or down, without an owner realising. Being overweight is unhealthy, but it may take an outsider's remark to make an owner realise that there is a problem. Conversely, a drop in bodyweight may be the only pointer to an underlying problem.

The diseases against which dogs are vaccinated include:

ADENOVIRUS
Canine adenovirus 1 (CAV-1) affects the liver (hepatitis) and is seen within affected dogs as the classic 'blue eye', while CAV-2 is a cause of kennel cough (see later). Vaccines often include both canine adenoviruses.

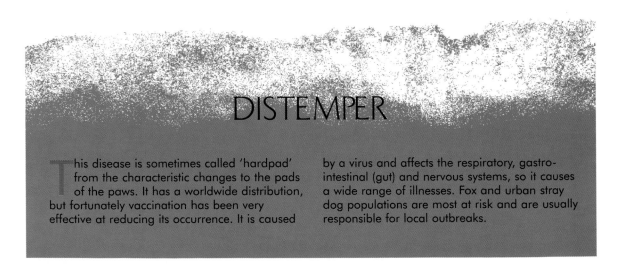

DISTEMPER

This disease is sometimes called 'hardpad' from the characteristic changes to the pads of the paws. It has a worldwide distribution, but fortunately vaccination has been very effective at reducing its occurrence. It is caused by a virus and affects the respiratory, gastro-intestinal (gut) and nervous systems, so it causes a wide range of illnesses. Fox and urban stray dog populations are most at risk and are usually responsible for local outbreaks.

Kennel Cough will spread rapidly among dogs that live together.

KENNEL COUGH

Kennel cough can seem alarming. There is a persistent cough accompanied by the production of white frothy spittle, which can last for a matter of weeks; during this time the patient is highly infectious to other dogs. I remember when it ran through our five Border Collies – there were white patches of froth on the floor wherever you looked! Other features include sneezing, a runny nose, and eyes sore with conjunctivitis. Fortunately, these infections are generally self-limiting, most dogs recovering without any long-lasting problems, but a young puppy or an elderly dog may be knocked sideways by it.

Also known as **infectious tracheobronchitis**, *Bordetella bronchiseptica* is not only a major cause of kennel cough but also a common secondary infection on top of another cause. Being a bacterium, it is susceptible to treatment with appropriate antibiotics, but the immunity stimulated by the vaccine is therefore short-lived (6-12 months).

This vaccine is often in a form to be administered down the nostrils in order to stimulate local immunity at the point of entry, so to speak. Do not be alarmed to see your veterinary surgeon using a needle and syringe to draw up the vaccine, because the needle will be replaced with a special plastic introducer, allowing the vaccine to be gently instilled into each nostril. Dogs generally resent being held more than the actual intra-nasal vaccine, and I have learnt that covering the patient's eyes helps greatly.

Kennel cough is, however, rather a catch-all term for any cough spreading within a dog population – not just in kennels, but also between dogs at a training session or breed show, or even mixing in the park. Many of these infections may not be *B. bronchiseptica* but other viruses, for which one can only treat symptomatically. **Parainfluenza** virus is often included in a vaccine programme, as it is a common viral cause of kennel cough.

LEPTOSPIROSIS

Leptospirosis is a zoonotic disease, known as Weil's disease in humans, with implications for all those in contact with an affected dog. The common way that dogs contract the disease is through contact with rats and their urine. As the rat population is high across the country, there is an equal risk of the Dachshund picking up the disease in town and country.

The illness in a susceptible dog may be mild, with the dog recovering within two to three weeks without treatment but going on to develop long-term liver or kidney disease. In contrast, an initial malaise and fever may be followed by rapid deterioration and death.

In the UK, annual vaccination is recommended for leptospirosis because the immunity only lasts for a year. The situation in America is less clear-cut and blanket vaccination against leptospirosis is not considered necessary because it only occurs in certain areas. You must be guided by your veterinarian's knowledge of the local situation.

PARVOVIRUS (CPV)
Canine parvovirus disease first appeared in the late 1970s, when it was feared that the UK's dog population would be decimated by it because of the lack of immunity in the general canine population. While this was a terrifying possibility at the time, fortunately it did not happen.

There are two forms of the virus (CPV-1, CPV-2) affecting domesticated dogs. It is highly contagious, picked up via the mouth/nose from infected faeces. The incubation period is about five days. Infection of puppies under three weeks of age with CPV-1 manifests as diarrhoea, vomiting, difficulty breathing, and fading puppy syndrome. CPV-1 can cause abortion and foetal abnormalities in breeding bitches. CPV-2 causes two types of illness: gastro-enteritis and heart disease in puppies born to unvaccinated dams, both of which often result in death.

Occurrence is mainly low now, thanks to vaccination, although a recent outbreak in my area did claim the lives of several puppies and dogs. It is also occasionally seen in the elderly unvaccinated dog.

RABIES
This is another zoonotic disease and there are very strict control measures in place. Under the Pet Travel Scheme (PETS), provided certain criteria are met (check the DEFRA website for up-to-date information – www.defra.gov.uk), dogs can re-enter the UK without being quarantined.

Dogs to be imported into the USA have to show that they were vaccinated against rabies at least 30 days previously; otherwise, they have to serve effective internal quarantine for 30 days from the date of vaccination

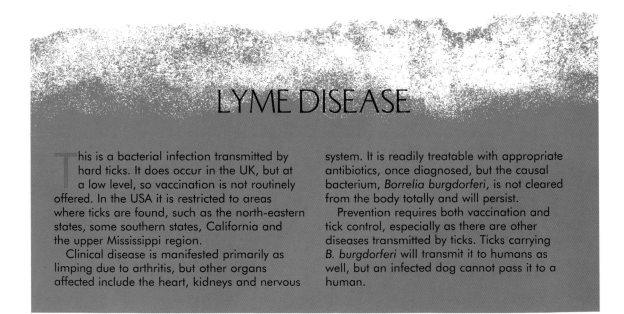

LYME DISEASE

This is a bacterial infection transmitted by hard ticks. It does occur in the UK, but at a low level, so vaccination is not routinely offered. In the USA it is restricted to areas where ticks are found, such as the north-eastern states, some southern states, California and the upper Mississippi region.

Clinical disease is manifested primarily as limping due to arthritis, but other organs affected include the heart, kidneys and nervous system. It is readily treatable with appropriate antibiotics, once diagnosed, but the causal bacterium, *Borrelia burgdorferi*, is not cleared from the body totally and will persist.

Prevention requires both vaccination and tick control, especially as there are other diseases transmitted by ticks. Ticks carrying *B. burgdorferi* will transmit it to humans as well, but an infected dog cannot pass it to a human.

against rabies, in order to ensure they are not incubating the disease. The exception is dogs entering from countries recognised as being rabies-free, in which case it has to be proved that they lived in that country for at least six months beforehand.

PARASITES

A parasite is an organism deriving benefit, on a one-way basis, from a host. A dog could harbour parasites, internal and/or external, without there being any signs apparent to the owner. Many canine parasites can, however, transfer to humans with variable consequences, so routine preventative treatment is advised.

Just as with vaccination, risk assessment plays a part – for example, there is no need for routine heartworm treatment in the UK (at present), but it is vital in the USA and in Mediterranean countries.

ROUNDWORM (NEMATODES)

These are the spaghetti-like worms that you may see passed in faeces or brought up in vomit. Most of the deworming treatments in use today cause the adult roundworms to disintegrate, thankfully, so that treating puppies in particular is not as unpleasant as it used to be!

Most puppies will have a worm burden, mainly of a particular roundworm species (*Toxocara canis*), which reactivates within the dam's tissues during pregnancy and passes to the foetuses developing in the womb.

Most puppies will carry a burden of roundworm.

It is therefore important to treat the dam both during and after pregnancy, as well as the puppies.

Professional advice is to continue worming every one to three months and there are deworming products that are active all the time, which will provide continuous protection when administered as often as directed.

TAPEWORMS (CESTODES)

When considering the general dog population, the primary source of the commonest tapeworm species will be fleas, which can carry the eggs. Most multi-wormers will be active against tapeworms. They are not a threat to human health, but it is unpleasant to see the wriggly rice-grain tapeworm segments

emerging from your dog's back passage while he is lying in front of the fire, and usually when you have guests for dinner!

There are specific requirements for treatment with praziquantel within 24 to 48 hours of a dog returning to the UK under the PETS. This is to prevent the introduction of *Echinococcus multilocularis*, a tapeworm carried by foxes on mainland Europe, which is transmissible to humans, causing serious or even fatal liver disease.

HEARTWORM (DIROFILARIA IMMITIS)

Heartworm infection has been diagnosed in dogs all over the world. There are two prerequisites: the presence of mosquitoes, and a warm, humid climate.

Heartworm infection is not currently a problem in the UK, except for those dogs contracting it while abroad without suitable preventative treatment. It is a potentially life-threatening condition, with dogs of all breeds and ages being susceptible without preventative treatment.

In the USA, regular blood tests for the presence of infection are advised, coupled with appropriate preventative measures, so I would advise liaison with your veterinary surgeon. For dogs travelling to heartworm-endemic areas of the EU, such as the Mediterranean coast, preventative treatment should be started before leaving the UK and maintained during the visit.

Adults should be routinely wormed throughout their lives.

FLEAS

There are several species of flea, which are not host-specific. A dog can be carrying cat and human fleas as well as dog fleas, but the same flea treatment will kill and/or control them all. Environmental control is a vital part of a flea control programme because the adult flea is only on your dog for as long as it takes to have a blood meal and to breed; the remainder of the life-cycle occurs in the house, car, caravan, shed, or elsewhere.

There is a vast array of flea control products available, with various routes of administration: collar, powder, spray, 'spot-on', or oral. Flea control needs to be applied to all pets in the house, regardless of whether they leave the house, since fleas can be introduced into the home by other pets and their human owners. Discuss your specific flea control needs with your veterinary surgeon.

MITES

There are five types of mite that can affect dogs:

Demodex canis: This mite is a normal inhabitant of canine hair follicles, passed from the bitch to her pups as they suckle. The development of actual skin disease or demodicosis depends on the individual. Some Dachshunds may develop the generalised form of demodicosis for the first time in middle-age (more than four years of age).

Sarcoptes scabei: This characteristically causes an intense pruritus or itchiness in the affected Dachshund, causing him to scratch incessantly and bite at himself, leading to marked fur loss and skin trauma. Initially starting on the elbows, earflaps and hocks, without treatment the skin on the rest of the body can become affected, with thickening and pigmentation of the skin.

Cheyletiella yasguri: This is the fur mite most commonly found on dogs. It is often called 'walking dandruff' because it can be possible to see collections of the small white mite moving about over the skin surface.

Otodectes cynotis: A highly transmissible otitis externa (outer ear infection) results from the presence in the outer ear canal of this ear mite, characterised by exuberant production of dark earwax. The patient will frequently shake his head and rub at the ear(s) affected. The mites can also spread on to the skin adjacent to the opening of the external ear canal, and may transfer elsewhere, such as to the paws.

(Neo-) Trombicula autumnalis: The free-living harvest mite can cause an intense local irritation on the skin. Its larvae are picked up from undergrowth, so they are characteristically found as a bright orange patch on the web of skin between the digits of the paws. It feeds on skin cells before dropping off to complete its life cycle in the environment.

Your veterinary surgeon will be able to diagnose and recommend suitable treatments for each of these types of mite.

Regular grooming will ensure you spot any signs of external parasites.

TICKS
Ticks have become an increasing problem in recent years throughout Britain. Rough, long grass is a major habitat. Their physical presence causes irritation, but it is their potential to spread disease, such as Lyme disease, that causes concern.

Removing a tick is simple – provided your dog will stay still. The important rule is to twist gently so that the tick is persuaded to let go with its mouth-parts. Grasp the body of the tick as near to your dog's skin as possible, either between thumb and fingers or with a specific tick-removing instrument, and then rotate in one direction until the tick comes away.

A-Z OF COMMON AILMENTS

ANAL SACS (IMPACTED)
The anal sacs lie on either side of the anus at approximately four and eight o'clock, if compared with the face of a clock. They fill with a particularly pungent fluid, which is emptied on to the faeces as they move past the sacs to exit from the anus. Theories abound as to why these sacs should become impacted periodically and seemingly more so in some dogs than others.

The irritation of impacted anal sacs is often seen as 'scooting', when the backside is dragged along the ground. Some dogs will also gnaw at their back feet or over the rump.

Increasing the fibre content of the diet helps some dogs; in others, there is underlying skin disease. It may be a one-off occurrence for no apparent reason. Sometimes an infection can become established, requiring antibiotic therapy, which may need to be coupled with flushing out the infected sac under sedation or general anaesthesia. More rarely, a dog will present with an apparently acute-onset anal sac abscess, which is incredibly painful.

DIARRHOEA
Cause and treatment much as **G**astritis (see below).

EAR INFECTIONS
The dog has a long external ear canal, initially vertical then horizontal, leading to the eardrum, which protects the middle ear. If your Dachshund is shaking his head, then his ears will need to be inspected with an auroscope by a veterinary surgeon in order to identify any cause and to ensure the eardrum is intact. A sample may be taken from the canal to be examined under the microscope and cultured, to identify causal agents before prescribing appropriate eardrops containing antibiotic,

antifungal agent and/or steroid. Predisposing causes of otitis externa or infection in the external ear canal include:

- Presence of a foreign body, such as a grass awn
- Ear mites, which are intensely irritating to the dog and stimulate the production of brown wax, predisposing to infection
- Previous infections, causing the canal's lining to thicken, narrowing the canal and reducing ventilation
- Bathing and swimming – water trapped in the external ear canal can lead to infection, especially if the water is not clean.

The older dog may be a little stiff after exercise.

FOREIGN BODIES

Internal: Items swallowed in haste without checking whether they will be digested can cause problems if they lodge in the stomach or obstruct the intestines, necessitating surgical removal. Acute vomiting is the main sign. Common objects I have seen removed include stones from the garden, peach stones, babies' dummies, golf balls and, once, a lady's bra… It is possible to diagnose a dog with an intestinal obstruction across a waiting room from a particularly 'tucked-up' stance and pained facial expression.

These patients bounce back from surgery dramatically. A previously docile and compliant obstructed patient will return for a post-operative check-up and literally bounce into the consulting room.

External: Grass awns are adept at finding their way into orifices such as a nostril, down an ear, and into the soft skin between two digits (toes), whence they start a one-way journey due to the direction of their whiskers. In particular, I remember a grass awn that migrated from a hind paw, causing abscesses along the way but not yielding itself up until it erupted through the skin in the groin!

GASTRITIS

This is usually a simple stomach upset, most commonly in response to dietary indiscretion.

Scavenging constitutes a change in the diet as much as an abrupt switch in the food being fed by the owner.

There are also some specific infections causing more severe gastritis/enteritis, which will require treatment from a veterinary surgeon (see also **Canine Parvovirus** under 'Vaccination').

Generally, a day without food, followed by a few days of small, frequent meals of a bland diet (such as cooked chicken or fish), or an appropriate prescription diet, should allow the stomach to settle. It is vital to ensure the patient is drinking and retaining sufficient water to cover losses resulting from the stomach upset, in addition to the normal losses to be expected when healthy. Oral rehydration fluid may not be very appetising for the patient, in which case cooled boiled water should be offered. Fluids should initially be offered in small but frequent amounts to avoid over-drinking, which can result in further vomiting and thereby dehydration and electrolyte imbalances. It is also important to wean the patient back on to routine food gradually or else another bout of gastritis may occur.

JOINT PROBLEMS

It is not unusual for older Dachshunds to be stiff after exercise, particularly in cold weather. This is not really surprising, given that they are such busy dogs when young. This is such a game breed that a nine or 10-year-old Dachshund will not readily forego an extra walk or take kindly to turning for home earlier than usual. Your veterinary surgeon will be able to advise you on ways of helping your dog cope with stiffness, not least of which will be to ensure that he is not overweight. Arthritic joints do not need to be burdened with extra bodyweight!

LUMPS

Regularly handling and stroking your dog will enable the early detection of lumps and bumps. These may be due to infection (abscess), bruising, multiplication of particular cells from within the body, or even an external parasite (tick). If you are worried about any lump you find, have it checked by a veterinary surgeon.

OBESITY

Being overweight does predispose to many other problems, such as diabetes

Teeth cleaning will reduce the risk of gum infection and tooth decay.

mellitus, heart disease and joint problems. It is so easily prevented by simply acting as your Dachshund's conscience. Ignore pleading eyes and feed according to your dog's waistline. The body condition is what matters qualitatively, alongside monitoring his bodyweight as a quantitative measure. The Dachshund should, in my opinion as a health professional, have at least a suggestion of a waist and it should be possible to feel the ribs beneath only a slight layer of fat.

Neutering does not automatically mean that your Dachshund will be overweight. Having an ovario-hysterectomy does slow down the body's rate of working, castration to a lesser extent, but it therefore means that your dog needs less food. I

recommend cutting back a little on the amount of food fed a few weeks before spaying to accustom your Dachshund to less food. If a bitch looks a little underweight on the morning of the operation, it will help the veterinary surgeon as well as giving her a little leeway weight-wise afterwards. It is always harder to lose weight after neutering than before, because of this slowing in the body's inherent metabolic rate.

TEETH PROBLEMS

Eating food starts with the canine teeth gripping and killing prey in the wild, incisor teeth biting off pieces of food, and the molar teeth chewing it. To be able to eat is vital for life, yet the actual health of the teeth is often overlooked: unhealthy teeth can predispose to disease, and not just by reducing the ability to eat. The presence of infection within the mouth can lead to bacteria entering the bloodstream and then filtering out at major organs, with potentially serious consequences. That is not to forget that simply having dental pain can affect a dog's well-being, as anyone who has had toothache will confirm.

Veterinary dentistry has made huge leaps in recent years, so that it no longer consists of extraction as the treatment of necessity. Good dental health lies in the hands of the owner, starting from the moment the dog comes into your care. Just as we have taken on responsibility for feeding, so we have acquired the task of maintaining good dental and oral hygiene. In an ideal world, we should brush our dogs' teeth as regularly as our own, but the Dachshund puppy who finds having his teeth brushed is a huge game and excuse to roll over and over on the ground requires lots of patience.

There are alternative strategies, ranging from dental chew-sticks to specially formulated foods, but the main thing is to be aware of your dog's mouth. At least train your puppy to permit full examination of his teeth. This will not only ensure you can check his mouth regularly but will also make your veterinary surgeon's job easier when there is a real need for your dog to 'open wide!'

INHERITED DISORDERS

Any individual, dog or human, may have an inherited disorder by virtue of the genes acquired from the parents. This is significant not only for the health of that individual but also because of the potential for transmitting the disorder on to that individual's offspring and to subsequent generations, depending on the mode of inheritance.

There are control schemes in place for some inherited disorders in Dachshunds. In the UK there are formal KC/BVA schemes in place for particular eye conditions. In the USA, the Canine Eye Registration Foundation (CERF) provides a database of dogs who have been examined by diplomates of the American College of Veterinary Ophthalmologists.

To date, a few conditions have been confirmed in the Dachshund varieties as being hereditary. However, that does not mean that they are

widespread, or common, and you should consult a breed club, or the breed council's website, for the most up-to-date information on known health problems. In alphabetical order, known hereditary conditions include:

CONGENITAL DEAFNESS

Dachshunds with two dapple-coloured parents (so-called 'double dapples') have an increased chance of congenital deafness, which can occur in one or both ears. A unilaterally deaf Dachshund can hear in one ear only, which means he knows that you are calling him but is unable to locate your position so he will scan until he finds you visually. This problem used to be called directional deafness. It is now possible to assess a puppy's hearing accurately from the age of five weeks, using the BAER (brainstem auditory evoked response) test. Note that 'double-dapples' are also more prone to eye defects.

Responsible breeders would not mate dapple to dapple, and since January 2010 the Kennel Club in the UK no longer registers puppies born from two dapple parents.

CRYPTORCHIDISM

During foetal development, the testicles form high within the abdomen and move down through the abdomen, out along the inguinal canal, and into their final position in the scrotum. A dog is said to be cryptorchid if

The aim is to breed Dachshunds without exaggeration.

LAFORA'S DISEASE

This is a relatively new disease found in Miniature Wire-haired Dachshunds in which clinical signs do not become apparent until later in life, usually from five years of age onwards. It is an inherited late-onset and progressive form of epilepsy affecting some Miniature Wire-haired Dachshunds and characterised by jerking and shuddering of the head in a backward direction. Common triggers include flashing lights, sudden movements near the head and unexpected noises. It can also occur during sleep. Some affected Dachshunds may also start having the more usual type of epileptic fits as well.

A gene mutation has been identified as being responsible for Lafora's disease, which is inherited in an autosomal recessive fashion.

There isn't a full DNA test available as yet, but hopefully a DNA test will be available soon and a screening programme is planned for the UK in 2010.

Diagnosis is based upon the clinical picture and can be confirmed by examining biopsies from liver (most reliable source), muscle or nerve tissue.

Early in the disease, feeding a diet with a low glycaemic index and avoiding carbohydrate-rich treats may help. Avoiding sunlight, and even wearing sunglasses, has been found useful for some dogs. If an individual develops epilepsy, management can be quite problematic, requiring different drug regimes from standard anti-epileptic treatments.

one (colloquially: 'monorchid') or both testicles is absent from the scrotum and is instead located within the inguinal canal or within the abdomen. In the Dachshund, this may be inherited in an autosomal recessive fashion.

DERMOIDS

A dermoid is a flap of normal skin growing on the cornea or conjunctiva of the eye. Larger dermoids may irritate the eye and reduce the field of vision, necessitating removal.

DISTICHIASIS

The Miniature Long-haired Dachshund is predisposed to the growth of an extra row of eyelashes, which rub on the cornea. Signs will vary according to the number and location of the extra eyelashes, and include soreness, weepy eyes, infections and an increased blink rate. Treatment ranges from simply plucking the extra eyelashes (which will re-grow) to surgery.

ENDOCRINE DISORDERS

There may be an increased risk of hypothyroidism (underactive thyroid), Cushing's syndrome (hyperadrenocorticism) and diabetes mellitus in the Dachshund.

ENTROPION

This is an in-rolling of the eyelids. There are degrees of entropion, ranging from a slight in-rolling to the more serious case, requiring surgical correction because of the pain and damage to the surface of the eyeball.

GENERALISED PROGRESSIVE RETINAL ATROPHY (gPRA - cord1)

Degeneration of both the rods and cones in the retina results in loss of vision. In Dachshunds (and English Springer Spaniels) the cones degenerate before the rods, which is why their form of GPRA is called "cord1". The

Animal Health Trust has investigated the genetic basis for GPRA-cord1 and identified a mutation in one particular gene causing GPRA-cord1 in Miniature Long-haired and Miniature Smooth-haired Dachshunds. The age of onset can be as young as six months, but it has also been first identified in much older individuals, or in some cases may not even become apparent during an individual's lifetime. The availability of the 'cord1' DNA test means that it is now possible to test a cheek swab for this particular form of GPRA before there are clinical signs of the disease. The breed clubs and KC advise that all breeding stock should be tested before mating.

INTERVERTEBRAL DISC DISEASE (IVDD)

The Dachshund's characteristically short, thick limbs result from abnormal development of the cartilage. This can, however, also affect the intervertebral discs that lie between the bodies of the vertebrae of the bony spine to act as shock absorbers so that they are less able to contain the nucleus and prevent it from herniating into the spinal canal.

Type 1 IVDD typically first occurs in the Dachshund between four and seven years of age. Several intervertebral discs may be affected. There is a sudden onset of pain; other effects - such as weakness,

Increasingly owners are becoming aware of the benefit of complementary therapies.

incoordination, lameness or paralysis, sensation defects and loss of control over bladder and bowels - are variable, depending on the area of the spinal cord affected and the degree of compression. Diagnosis is often initially presumptive, based on the sudden onset of these clinical signs in a young Dachshund.

Left untreated, there is the real possibility of permanent paralysis and incontinence. There can be a good response to pain relief and cage rest, but surgical treatment to relieve the pressure on the spinal cord is often required. The success of surgery depends on a range of factors, such as the time between onset of clinical signs and surgery, the nature and severity of the effects of spinal cord compression and the presence or absence of deep pain sensation.

MITRAL VALVE DISEASE (MVD)

Some Dachshunds show a predisposition to the early

development of MVD and congestive heart failure. Blood leaking back through the mitral valve can be heard as a murmur when a stethoscope is placed on the chest wall, especially over the valve, so that a common time to first suspect MVD is during a routine examination by a veterinary surgeon.

Clinical signs of congestive heart failure, such as a reduced ability to exercise, breathlessness and a cough at night or after resting, may not become apparent for some years after first detecting a mitral valve heart murmur. A detailed ultrasound examination is needed to diagnose and gauge the extent of the problem.

OPTIC NERVE HYPOPLASIA (ONH)

This is a congenital condition where the optic nerve fails to develop, consequently causing blindness in one or both eyes. It is controlled in the Miniature Long-haired Dachshund under Schedule B of the BVA/KC/ISDS Scheme* in the UK.

PERSISTENT PUPILLARY MEMBRANE

This condition of the eyes is monitored in the Miniature Wire-haired Dachshund under Schedule B of the BVA/KC/ISDS Scheme in the UK.

SICK SINUS SYNDROME

This is a heart condition sometimes found in older Dachshunds who may faint or have episodes of weakness. The heart rate is slower than usual and does not show the usual increase one would expect on exercising. On running an ECG, there are signs of a disordered heart rhythm. Treatment may not be necessary if an individual is only mildly affected. There are drugs available for those having frequent fainting episodes, who ultimately might have a pacemaker fitted.

ACANTHOSIS NIGRICANS

Darkening of the skin due to an accumulation of the pigment melanin is a common occurrence following skin disease, but it is inherited in the Dachshund as a pigmentation disorder in its own right. It is relatively uncommon.

This condition cannot be cured, but it can be managed with appropriate shampoos and treatment of secondary infections as they occur.

PATTERN BALDNESS (PINNAL ALOPECIA)

In the Dachshund, the male is more commonly affected than bitches, with hair loss from the ears starting before the age of one year. There is no discomfort

With good care and management, your Dachshund should live a long, happy and healthy life.

and the remaining coat is normal. Once diagnosed, by excluding other causes of hair loss, there is no treatment available to reverse the baldness.

COMPLEMENTARY THERAPIES

Just as for human health, I do believe that there is a place for alternative therapies alongside and complementing orthodox treatment under the supervision of a veterinary surgeon. That is why 'complementary therapies' is a better name.

Because animals do not have a choice, there are measures in place to safeguard their well-

being and welfare. All manipulative treatment must be under the direction of a veterinary surgeon who has examined the patient and diagnosed the condition that he or she feels needs that form of treatment.

SUMMARY

As the owner of a Dachshund, you are responsible for his care and health. Not only must you make decisions on his behalf, you are also responsible for establishing a lifestyle for him that will ensure he leads a long and happy life. Diet plays an important part in this, as does exercise.

Please do not look through this chapter and worry about all the things that could happen. As I said at the start of this chapter, Dachshunds are generally a very stoic, healthy and long-lived breed of dog. The conditions described here are for your guidance and the majority could apply to any dog, whether pedigree or crossbreed. Always speak to your veterinary surgeon if you have any worries about your Dachshund.

It is important to remember that your Dachshund has no choice. As his owner, you are responsible for any decision made, so it must be as informed a decision as possible. He is not just a dog: from the moment you brought him home, he became a member of the family.

THE CONTRIBUTORS

JOINT EDITOR:
JUDY SQUIRES (WIREHALL)

Judy and husband Peter share their home with five Miniature Wires with the "Wirehall" affix and although she does not exhibit any more she is kept busy "doing her bit" for the Dachshund world. She has a particular interest in health matters as she is on the Health and Welfare Sub-committee of the Breed Council.

Judy is a member of the Kennel Club and a long-term Committee member of the Eastern Counties Dachshund Association and President of The Miniature Dachshund Club after being Chairman for a number of years.

She started judging in 1982 and gained Championship Judge status in 1991. She now awards Challenge Certificates in all six varietes of Dachshund.

Judy has a long-term affection for Dachshunds, especially the Miniature Wires, and by working for the Dachshund Clubs hopes she is putting something back for all the enjoyment and fun that she has had from successfully breeding and showing her Wirehall Miniature Wires over the last thirty years.

See Chapter One: Getting to know the Dachshund, Chapter Three: A Dachshund for your lifestyle.

JOINT EDITOR:
IAN SEATH (SUNSONG)

Ian has owned Dachshunds, with his wife Sue, since 1980. They started with a pair of Miniature Long-haired dogs which Sue was persuaded to show. In 1982 they bought their first Wire-haired Dachshund and today, they show the "Sunsong" Miniature Smooth-haired and Wire-haired Dachshunds.

In the 1980s he learnt the skills of running dog shows as Show Manager for Basingstoke and District Canine Society where he managed two general Open Shows each year, for several years. He has served on the committees of the Wirehaired Dachshund Club, Southern Dachshund Association (as Treasurer and then Chairman) and Eastern Counties Dachshund Association (as Secretary).

In 2008 Ian was elected as the first Chairman of the newly formed Dachshund Breed Council, representing the interests of all nineteen Dachshund Clubs. His particular interests are Dachshund health and welfare and the education and training of judges.

Ian also judges Dachshunds at Championship Show level, first awarding Challenge Certificates in 2000.

See Chapter Four: The New Arrival, Chapter Five: Caring for your Dachshund, Chapter Seven: The Perfect Dachshund.

ZENA THORN-ANDREWS (DRAKESLEAT)

Zena first showed her Irish Wolfhound in 1968, and her first home-bred Miniature Wirehaired Dachshund in 1970. Both became famous champions. Since those days her Drakesleat kennel has been responsible for 118 British Champions, of which 97 are M/W Dachshunds.

She is the first person in any breed, to own or breed 100 Champions since records began in 1873. The hounds have won well over 700 Challenge Certificates, over 40 groups and many all-breed Best in Shows. The first and only Min Wire Best in Show winner was owned in partnership by the kennel and both breed record holders in Irish Wolfhounds and Min Wires were bred by Zena under the Drakesleat affix.

Zena is an FCI all-breed judge and is currently the only judge in the UK who is passed to award Challenge Certificates in every breed. She has a vast collection of early dog books and enjoys studying the history of all breeds. She holds several honorary positions in various breed clubs.

See Chapter Two: History.

ANN GORDON (RAVENRIDGE, USA)

Ann Gordon has been involved with Dachshunds for over fifty years. During twenty of those years, she bred and showed standard smooth Dachshunds in conformation competition under the kennel name of Ravenridge.

Over the many years that she has been a member of the Dachshund Club of America, Ann has served in the capacity of 2nd Vice-President, 1st Vice-President, and as a member of the Board of Directors. She was the DCA Judges Education Coordinator for several years and continues to serve as a member of the Judges Education Committee.

Ann is the Dachshund breed columnist for the *AKC Gazette*, and has been writing the column for more than twenty years. She has written a book on the Dachshund titled, *The Dachshund, A Dog for Town and Country*, which was published in 2000 by Howell Book House. She did the revision for the 2nd Edition of the *Dachshund* in the Howell Book House *Your Happy Healthy Pet* series published in 2005.

See Chapter Two: History - USA.

DEREK SMITH (CLICKAM)

Derek began in the dog world in the 1950s and his first champion Collie was born in 1959. Since then, many champions have followed. Today, in partnership with Steve and Alison Barrett, a large kennel is maintained. The current star is Ch. Brooklyn Son from Rio who has 20 CCs and won Groups and BIS at Championship Shows.

During the 1970s Derek showed Longhaired Dachshunds under the Frankanwen Affix of Wendy Barrow. Again, many Champions, Group and BIS winners emerged.

Derek started his judging career in 1964, attaining championship status in 1972 and now awards CCs to 24 breeds across four Groups. He judges Working, Pastoral and Utility Groups and BIS at Championship level. He has had the honour of judging at Crufts fourteen times; the Pastoral Group in 2002 and the Working Group in 2004.

See Chapter Two: History – Influential UK Dachshunds.

SUE SEATH (SUNSONG)

Sue has owned, shown and bred Dachshunds for 30 years, starting with Mini Longs in 1980, then Wires from 1982 and Mini Smooths from 1999. During this time she has bred one Champion - Sunsong Witching Hour who was crowned at Crufts in 1995 - and fifteen others that have won Challenge Certificates or Reserve CCs.

The Sunsong kennel has imported Wires from Iceland and America to strengthen their breeding programme and widen the gene pool. Their American import Stonevale Stars and Stripes at Sunsong has been a successful sire, producing several puppies that have won CCs or RCCs and grand-children that have been similarly successful.

Sue has judged Dachshunds since 1987 and awards Challenge Certificates in all six varieties.

See Chapter Four: The New Arrival.

EDNA COOPER (SONTAG)

Edna has owned Smooth Haired Dachshunds since 1969. It has always been her only variety and she bought her first bitch purely as a pet.

Over the years Edna has won various top awards for Smooth Breeder, Puppy, Dog, Bitch and Stud Dog. Her current male, Ch. Sontag Simon le Bone JW, has been her most successful exhibit, Winning 17 CCs, 12 Res. CCs, several Best in Shows at Breed Club Championship and Breed Club Open Shows. He was top Smooth in '06 top male in '09 top sire in '08 and '09.

See Chapter One: Getting to know the Dachshund.

JEFF HORSWELL (DRAKESLEAT)

Jeff first began showing Min Wires in 1974, and has now made up 20 Champions in the variety. His most successful has been Ch. Drakesleat Toot Sweet, winner of 3 Hound Groups and BOB at Crufts, and Ch/Jap. Ch. Drakesleat JP Trier Winshoten, a group winner and with 18 CCs one of the top 3 males of all time.

He has also made up a Champion Greyhound and 2 Field Spaniel Show Champions. Jeff judges over 50 breeds with CCs in the UK in 6 groups as well as judging Best in Show. He has judged Dachshunds in Europe, America, Africa and Asia and is approved by the FCI as an all breeds judge.

Currently, Jeff is a member of the Dachshund Club committee, having previously held the position of Chairman.

See Chapter One: Getting to know the Dachshund.

FRAN MITCHELL (BRONIA)

Fran had her first Longhaired Dachshund in 1969 which she enjoyed showing at local sanction shows.

The Bronia kennel has now owned/bred 46 UK champions to date, in four different varieties, and Fran is very proud to have bred and owned the breed record holder for Longs, the well known Champion Bronia Conquistador, top winning Longhaired Dachshund in 1995, 96, 97 and 98 and Top Stud Dog in the breed history, siring 19 UK Champions.

See Chapter One: Getting to know the Dachshund.

SUE HOLT AND BERND KUGOW (WALDMEISTER)

Sue and Bernd have owned, bred, worked and shown Miniature Wire-haired Dachshunds since 1998.

To date, they have gained Junior Warrants, CCs and / or Reserve CCs with most of the ones they have shown. Sue has judged at Open Show level and has made up 3 Mini Wire Champions, achieved Best of Breed at Crufts in 2006 and Best Bitch and Reserve Best Bitch at Crufts 2009. Bernd is more interested in the working aspects and temperament of the breed.

See Chapter Six Training & Socialisation.

BRENDA HUMPHREY (SECRETARY, UK TECKEL STUD BOOK SOCIETY)

Brenda and Trevor Humphrey have owned working Teckels for 13 years. Their teckels have been successful in countries like America, Spain, Belgium, France and the UK for their working ability in finding dead or wounded deer. Ryeford Chase Bowe at Dewin Cymraeg and Dewin Cymraeg Zeta have been the most successful dogs that they have owned.

They are the joint founders of the UK Teckel Stud Book Society that was started in August 1999, together with Nick Valentine who is Master of Hounds with the Ryeford Chase pack. The Society provides facilities to record UK working Teckels, a puppy register and details of dogs available at stud.

See Chapter Six: Training & Socialisation.

LESLEY PATTON (LESANDNIC)

Lesley Patton has lived with Wire-haired Dachshunds since 1971. Over the years the Lesandnic kennel, started by her mother, have bred and/or made up numerous champions, including 11 UK champions, of which the best known would be Ch. Lesandnic Lucyrowe (16 CCs) and Ch. & Ir. Ch. Lesandnic Like A Butterfly (10 CCs, Group placings in UK & Ireland and Vitalin Bitch of The Year 2005).

Lesley also competes in obedience with her wires and the kennel have had 5 KC Good Citizen Wires, including the Gold GC Lesandnic Lizzy The Lizzard.

See Chapter One: Getting to know the Dachshund.

RUTH LOCKETT-WALTERS (RALINES)

Ruth's first introduction to Dachshunds was showing the Standard Smooth variety. She then acquired her first Mini Long which became a champion and she built her line of Ralines Dachhsunds on him.

Her three most famous dogs were Ch Ralines Royal Acclaim who won the Dachshund Club Jackdaw trophy for top Dachshund; her son Ch Ralines Royal Statesman who was top Hound Sire 2008 and his grandfather who was top Hound Sire in 2000. Ruth's Ralines kennel is the only Mini Long kennel to achieve this. Ruth has judged at Crufts twice and has had a total of 37 champions in the two varieties.

See Chapter One: Getting to know the Dachshund.

LOVAINE COXON (D'ARISCA)

Lovaine has owned and bred Smooth, Miniature Smooth and Wirehaired Dachshunds since 1959, she has also owned one miniature Longhaired during this time. Lovaine has produced many Smooth and Miniature Smooth champions. Some of them have gone on to win Best in Show at championship shows at breed level and also Best in Show at an all breeds championship show. This was with her Ch. D'Arisca Candice who achieved Top Winning Hound in the UK during her career.

Her current well known Ch. D'Arisca Golden Delicious has also won many awards including Reserve Best in Show at the Hound Association of Scotland Championship show. "Pippin" has produced two litters during her career and continues to be shown on a regular basis.

See Chapter One: Getting to know the Dachshund.

JULIA BARNES

Julia has owned and trained a number of different dog breeds, and has also worked as a puppy socialiser for Dogs for the Disabled. A former journalist, she has written many books, including several on dog training and behaviour. Julia is indebted to Sue Holt, Bernd Kugow, and Brenda Humphrey for their specialist knowledge about the different varieties of Dachshunds.

See Chapter Six: Training and Socialisation.

ALISON LOGAN MA VetMB MRCVS

Alison qualified as a veterinary surgeon from Cambridge University in 1989, having been brought up surrounded by all manner of animals and birds in the north Essex countryside. She has been in practice in her home town ever since, living with her husband, two children and Labrador Retriever Pippin.

She contributes on a regular basis to *Veterinary Times, Veterinary Nurse Times, Dogs Today, Cat World* and *Pet Patter*, the PetPlan newsletter. In 1995, Alison won the Univet Literary Award with an article on Cushing's Disease, and she won it again (as the Vetoquinol Literary Award) in 2002, writing about common conditions in the Shar-Pei.

See Chapter Eight: Happy and Healthy.

USEFUL ADDRESSES

KENNEL & BREED CLUBS

UK

The Kennel Club
1 Clarges Street, London, W1J 8AB
Tel: 0870 606 6750
Fax: 0207 518 1058
Web: www.the-kennel-club.org.uk

To obtain up-to-date contact information for the following breed clubs, please contact the Kennel Club:
• Cambrian Dachshund Club
• Dachshund Club
• Dachshund Club of Wales
• East Yorkshire Dachshund Club
• Eastern Counties Dachshund Association
• Lancashire & Cheshire Dachshund Club
• Long Haired Dachshund Club
• Midland Dachshund Club
• Miniature Dachshund Club
• North Eastern Dachshund Club
• Northern Dachshund Association
• Northern Long Haired Dachshund Breeders Association
• Scottish Dachshund Club
• Smooth Haired Dachshund Club
• Southern Dachshund Association
• Ulster Dachshund Club
• West of England Dachshund Club
• West Riding Dachshund Association
• Wire Haired Dachshund Club

Dachshund Breed Council
www.dachshundbreedcouncil.org.uk
www.uk-dachshund-health-report.org.uk

Dachshund Rescue
Contact Val Skinner (0114 284 7425) or Gill Goad (01458 850745)

USA

American Kennel Club (AKC)
5580 Centerview Drive,
Raleigh, NC 27606, USA.
Tel: 919 233 9767
Fax: 919 233 3627
Email: info@akc.org
Web: www.akc.org

United Kennel Club (UKC)
100 E Kilgore Rd, Kalamazoo,
MI 49002-5584, USA.
Tel: 269 343 9020
Fax: 269 343 7037
Web:www.ukcdogs.com/

Dachshund Club of America, Inc.
Membership Secretary Neal Hamilton,
59 Clover Hill Road, Flemington,
New Jersey 08822, USA.
Tel: 908 782 4724
Web: www.dachshund-dca.org/

For contact details of regional clubs, please contact Dachshund Club of America.

Dachshund Rescue Club of North America
www.drna.org/

AUSTRALIA
Australian National Kennel Council (ANKC)
The Australian National Kennel Council is the administrative body for pure breed canine affairs in Australia. It does not, however, deal directly with dog exhibitors, breeders or judges. For information pertaining to breeders, clubs or shows, please contact the relevant State or Territory Body.

Dogs Australian Capital Territory
PO Box 815, Dickson ACT 2602
Tel: (02) 6241 4404
Fax: (02) 6241 1129
Email: administrator@dogsact.org.au
Web: www.dogsact.org.au

Dogs New South Wales
PO Box 632, St Marys, NSW 1790
Tel: (02) 9834 3022 or 1300 728 022
Fax: (02) 9834 3872
Email: info@dogsnsw.org.au
Web: www.dogsnsw.org.au

Dogs Northern Territory
PO Box 37521, Winnellie NT 0821
Tel: (08) 8984 3570
Fax: (08) 8984 3409
Email: admin@dogsnt.com.au
Web: www.dogsnt.com.au

Dogs Queensland
PO Box 495, Fortitude Valley Qld 4006
Tel: (07) 3252 2661
Fax: (07) 3252 3864
Email: info@dogsqueensland.org.au
Web: www.dogsqueensland.org.au

Dogs South Australia
PO Box 844
Prospect East SA 5082
Tel: (08) 8349 4797
Fax: (08) 8262 5751
Email: info@dogssa.com.au
Web: www.dogssa.com.au

Tasmanian Canine Association Inc
The Rothman Building
PO Box 116
Glenorchy Tas 7010
Tel: (03) 6272 9443
Fax: (03) 6273 0844
Email: tca@iprimus.com.au
Web: www.tasdogs.com

Dogs Victoria
Locked Bag K9
Cranbourne VIC 3977
Tel: (03)9788 2500
Fax: (03) 9788 2599
Email: office@dogsvictoria.org.au
Web: www.dogsvictoria.org.au

Dogs Western Australia
PO Box 1404
Canning Vale WA 6970
Tel: (08) 9455 1188
Fax: (08) 9455 1190
Email: k9@dogswest.com
Web: www.dogswest.com
INTERNATIONAL

Fédération Cynologique Internationalé (FCI)/World Canine Organisation
Place Albert 1er, 13, B-6530 Thuin,
Belgium.
Tel: +32 71 59.12.38
Fax: +32 71 59.22.29
Web: www.fci.be/

Dachshund Rescue Australia
www.dachshundrescueaustralia.com/

TRAINING AND BEHAVIOUR

UK
Association of Pet Dog Trainers
PO Box 17, Kempsford, GL7 4WZ
Telephone: 01285 810811
Email: APDToffice@aol.com
Web: http://www.apdt.co.uk

Association of Pet Behaviour Counsellors
PO BOX 46, Worcester, WR8 9YS
Telephone: 01386 751151
Fax: 01386 750743
Email: info@apbc.uk
Web: http://www.apbc.org.uk/

USA
Association of Pet Dog Trainers
101 North Main Street, Suite 610
Greenville, SC 29601, USA.
Tel: 1 800 738 3647
Email: information@apdt.com
Web: www.apdt.com/

American College of Veterinary Behaviorists
College of Veterinary Medicine, 4474 Tamu, Texas A&M University
College Station, Texas 77843-4474
Web: http://dacvb.org/

American Veterinary Society of Animal Behavior
Web: www.avsabonline.org/

AUSTRALIA

APDT Australia Inc
PO Box 3122, Bankstown Square, NSW 2200, Australia.
Email: secretary@apdt.com.au
Web: www.apdt.com.au

Canine Behaviour
For details of regional behaviourists, contact the relevant State or Territory Controlling Body.

ACTIVITIES

UK
Agility Club
http://www.agilityclub.co.uk/

British Flyball Association
PO Box 990, Doncaster, DN1 9FY
Telephone: 01628 829623
Email: secretary@flyball.org.uk
Web: http://www.flyball.org.uk/

DACHSHUND

USA

North American Dog Agility Council
P.O. Box 1206, Colbert,
OK 74733, USA.
Web: www.nadac.com/

North American Flyball Association, Inc.
1333 West Devon Avenue, #512
Chicago, IL 60660
Tel/Fax: 800 318 6312
Email: flyball@flyball.org
Web: www.flyball.org/

AUSTRALIA

Agility Dog Association of Australia
ADAA Secretary, PO Box 2212,
Gailes, QLD 4300, Australia.
Tel: 0423 138 914
Email: admin@adaa.com.au
Web: www.adaa.com.au/

NADAC Australia (North American Dog Agility Council - Australian Division)
12 Wellman Street, Box Hill South, Victoria 3128, Australia.
Email: shirlene@nadacaustralia.com
Web: www.nadacaustralia.com/

Australian Flyball Association
PO Box 4179, Pitt Town, NSW 2756
Tel: 0407 337 939
Email: info@flyball.org.au
Web: www.flyball.org.au/

INTERNATIONAL

World Canine Freestyle Organisation
P.O. Box 350122, Brooklyn, NY 11235-2525, USA
Tel: (718) 332-8336
Fax: (718) 646-2686
Email: wcfodogs@aol.com
Web: www.worldcaninefreestyle.org

HEALTH

UK

Alternative Veterinary Medicine Centre
Chinham House, Stanford in the Vale,
Oxfordshire, SN7 8NQ
Tel: 01367 710324
Fax: 01367 718243
Web: www.alternativevet.org/

British Small Animal Veterinary Association
Woodrow House, 1 Telford Way,
Waterwells Business Park, Quedgeley,
Gloucestershire, GL2 2AB
Tel: 01452 726700
Fax: 01452 726701
Email: customerservices@bsava.com
Web: http://www.bsava.com/

Royal College of Veterinary Surgeons
Belgravia House, 62-64 Horseferry Road, London,
SW1P 2AF
Tel: 0207 222 2001
Fax: 0207 222 2004
Email: admin@rcvs.org.uk
Web: www.rcvs.org.uk

Animal Health Trust
www.aht.org.uk/

USA

American Holistic Veterinary Medical Association
2218 Old Emmorton Road
Bel Air, MD 21015
Tel: 410 569 0795
Fax 410 569 2346
Email: office@ahvma.org
Web: www.ahvma.org/

American Veterinary Medical Association
1931 North Meacham Road, Suite 100,
Schaumburg, IL 60173-4360, USA.
Tel: 800 248 2862
Fax: 847 925 1329
Web: www.avma.org

American College of Veterinary Surgeons
19785 Crystal Rock Dr, Suite 305
Germantown, MD 20874, USA.
Tel: 301 916 0200
Toll Free: 877 217 2287
Fax: 301 916 2287
Email: acvs@acvs.org
Web: www.acvs.org/

AUSTRALIA

Australian Holistic Vets
Web: www.ahv.com.au/

Australian Small Animal Veterinary Association
40/6 Herbert Street, St Leonards, NSW 2065,
Australia.
Tel: 02 9431 5090
Fax: 02 9437 9068
Email: asava@ava.com.au
Web: www.asava.com.au

Australian Veterinary Association
Unit 40, 6 Herbert Street, St Leonards, NSW
2065, Australia.
Tel: 02 9431 5000
Fax: 02 9437 9068
Web: www.ava.com.au

Australian College Veterinary Scientists
Building 3, Garden City Office Park,
2404 Logan Road, Eight Mile Plains, Queensland
4113, Australia.
Tel: 07 3423 2016
Fax: 07 3423 2977
Email: admin@acvs.org.au
Web: http://acvsc.org.au

ASSISTANCE DOGS

Canine Partners
Mill Lane, Heyshott, Midhurst,
, GU29 0ED
Tel: 08456 580480
Fax: 08456 580481
Web: www.caninepartners.co.uk

Dogs for the Disabled
The Frances Hay Centre, Blacklocks Hill,
Banbury, Oxon, OX17 2BS

Tel: 01295 252600
Web: www.dogsforthedisabled.org

Guide Dogs for the Blind Association
Burghfield Common, Reading, RG7 3YG
Tel: 01189 835555
Fax: 01189 835433
Web: www.guidedogs.org.uk/

Hearing Dogs for Deaf People
The Grange, Wycombe Road, Saunderton, Princes
Risborough, Bucks, HP27 9NS
Tel: 01844 348100
Fax: 01844 348101
Web: www.hearingdogs.org.uk

Pets as Therapy
3a Grange Farm Cottages, Wycombe Road,
Saunderton, Princes Risborough,
Bucks, HP27 9NS
Tel: 01845 345445
Fax: 01845 550236
Web: http://www.petsastherapy.org/

Support Dogs
21 Jessops Riverside, Brightside Lane, Sheffield, S9
2RX
Tel: 01142 617800
Fax: 01142 617555
Email: supportdogs@btconnect.com
Web: www.support-dogs.org.uk

USA

Therapy Dogs International
88 Bartley Road, Flanders, NJ 07836,.
Tel: 973 252 9800
Fax: 973 252 7171
Email: tdi@gti.net
Web: www.tdi-dog.o

Therapy Dogs Inc.
P.O. Box 20227, Cheyenne, WY 82003.
Tel: 307 432 0272.
Fax: 307-638-2079
Web: www.therapydogs.com

Delta Society - Pet Partners
875 124th Ave NE, Suite 101 • Bellevue, WA
98005 USA.
Email: info@DeltaSociety.org
Web: www.deltasociety.org

Comfort Caring Canines
8135 Lare Street, Philadelphia, PA 19128.
Email: ccc@comfortcaringcanines.org
Web: www.comfortcaringcanines.org/

AUSTRALIA

AWARE Dogs Australia, Inc
PO Box 883, Kuranda, Queensland, 488,
Australia.
Tel: 07 4093 8152
Web: www.awaredogs.org.au/

Delta Society — Therapy Dogs
Web: www.deltasociety.com.au